Points Of Life

Points Of Life

A Memoir and More

*To Anahid,
With my best wishes
Vartkes Kas
11/5/17*

Vartkes M. Kassouni

ISBN: 1542503671
ISBN 13: 9781542503679

Contents

Foreword

Rev. Dr. Vartkes Kassouni's memoir, *Points of Life*, has its beginning on the island of Cyprus where he grew up in a devout Armenian Evangelical family surrounded by a close-knit community of people from different denominations and religions. These differences, including the fact that as an evangelical he had to worship in a Presbyterian church with a different tradition than his own, formed the counterpoints that shaped his Christian faith and his commitment to seek his theological education in the United States. With the help of a spiritual mentor he came to the United States for his graduate studies at Bob Jones University in South Carolina. Young Vartkes's convictions about the plurality of life and accommodating those who were different did not change in spite of the University's strong fundamentalist orientation.

Rev. Kassouni's seminary studies at what is now New York Theological Seminary, and his ordination in the Armenian Evangelical Church of New York, brought him to the Armenian Evangelical community in the United States in which he served tirelessly for thirty-five years. His accomplishments in the starting of new churches, the revitalizing of those in decline, involvement in missionary work around the world, the assuming of leadership positions in the AEUNA (Armenian Evangelical Union of North America), and the promoting of the establishment of the first Armenian Evangelical school in the United States are aptly narrated in the memoirs. What stands out in all of these years is his continued participation in the mainstream Protestant community, in particular, the Presbyterian Church (USA).

The next twenty-six years were highlighted by Rev. Kassouni's pastorate in Presbyterian churches in Orange County and his appointment as associate executive presbyter that entailed developing new churches. His "Ecclesiastical Obstetrics" skills brought forth five new churches. It is during this time, and on the occasion of the one hundredth anniversary of the Armenian Genocide (1915–2015) that Rev. Kassouni, with the initiating support of Jinishian Memorial Program, and other Armenian clergy helped pass the overture in the General Assembly of the Presbyterian Church (USA), recognizing the Armenian Genocide and designating April 24 as the day for its observance in all its churches.

Rev. Kassouni's memoir is a painting of numerous colorful points and counterpoints knit together by a faith and theology that embrace others, serving them in word and deed. The humor and joy in presenting his lifelong career as pastor, leader, and teacher in Armenian Evangelical and American Presbyterian communities, while affirming his ethnic identity throughout, is unique.

Rev. Kassouni grew up on an island, nonetheless his entire life in the United States and abroad was a testimony that indeed "no man is an island." At a time when isolationism, sectarianism, and spiritual exclusivism are dominating our political and spiritual life, his memoirs are a source of hope that the understanding and acknowledgment of counterpoints to one's own position give life its fullness.

—Arthur Salibian, MD

Dedication

This book is dedicated to
my parents,
MANUEL AND MARTHA KASSOUNI,
whose love, devotion, wisdom,
and guidance provided the essential tenets
of my being.

Preface

Having reached the grand old age of eighty-six years, I have finally decided to publish my life story. I have done so in response to many who have asked, over the years, "When are you going to write a book?" Well, my friends, here it is.

My life's journey has been composed of a multitude of events, places, people, encounters, conversations, debates, relationships, thoughts, and beliefs. They have all somehow, by the grace of God, converged to form my person, and my destiny. Hence my use of the word "points" in the title. When I look back and ponder their number and their meaning, I am awed to silence. It is like when as a little boy, I used to sit on our back porch in Larnaca, Cyprus, on clear dark nights and gaze in utter amazement at the millions of stars in the sky. Consider me, then, to be not one of those stars but a shooting star that brightens the sky as it streaks across it for a moment or two and then disappears into oblivion!

Life's amazing dimensions include the positive and the negative, the beautiful and the ugly, the true and the false, the ups and the downs. Not only observing this but accepting it and incorporating it have been vitally necessary for the development of who I am, what my beliefs are, and how I am to carry on my life and mission in relation to others.[1]

In this book I have gathered significant events that have been milestones in my life journey. I have also included not-so-significant

---

1 See Appendix 1 for an article of mine titled, "Reflections and Convictions."

happenings which have, nevertheless, brought home to me the ironies, excitements, joys, and disappointments of life as teaching points. They have helped me to gain the perspectives without which my life would have remained isolated, dull, and insulated from a world beyond my immediate reach. Hence I have added "and more" to my "memoir."

The grand result of this life adventure in growth has been change. To the immature, change is a scary word, holding the prospects of giving up one's cherished way of life or way of belief in an increasingly alien world. To the mature, or to the process of maturing, it is welcomed as gates opening into new vistas or windows letting in fresh air. Counterpoints are understood and welcomed, not in rejection of the points one has held but in the affirming of truth that incorporates both. Ultimate truth resides in God alone, into whom our life journey is headed, and in whom all seeming contradictions are resolved.

In this book I have selected events and viewpoints that have been formative concerning my life, ministry, and relationships. Over thousands of sermons preached, classes taught, and articles written, I have come to a time when I seek to pass on my insights and values emanating from the experiences I've had. My life's focus has been the desire to pass on to others that which I received. It has been a fantastic gift, a treasure I cannot hoard. It has grown more precious and more fantastic with the passing of the years. For this I thank God, and countless people who have been God's channels to me.

St. John says, "In him (Christ) was life, and the life was the light of all people. The light shines in the darkness, and the darkness did not overcome it." Shine on, O light of God, shine on!
Vartkes M. Kassouni
January 1, 2017
Orange, California

One

BEGINNINGS

I've often asked myself, "Who am I?" In retrospect I've become aware that I am a child of terrible, fascinating, and exciting times. I am also a personality formed by a variety of different ethnic and religious communities. Foundational to it all is that my parents came from Turkey, having somehow survived the horrific years of Armenian genocide and World War I. They reunited in Larnaca, Cyprus and got married in a friend's house on March 20, 1922. My mother, Martha Mississian, came from Marash, and my father, Manuel Sarkis Kassouni, came from Aintab. They were both graduates of American mission schools: my mother from Central Turkey Girls College in Marash and my father from Central Turkey College in Aintab.

These were schools sponsored by the American Board of Commissioners for Foreign Missions (a mission board of the Congregational Church), and their influence in shaping my parents' faith, values, and outlook on life was profound. However, basic to it all was my father's rock-hard devotion to the Armenian people, including their language, culture, history, and future.

An episode that comes from his college years illustrates this. Aintab College's policy was to not allow the Armenian students to have any days off to celebrate their national holidays. This was done in deference to the Turkish authorities who forbade any expression of nationalism by the Armenian people. Well, my dad organized the students on a Vartanants Day that commemorated the battle of Avarair in AD 451. In that historic battle General Vartan Mamigonian led the Armenians, and lost his life, in a futile battle in defense of their Christian faith and homeland against overwhelming Persian forces. They stayed away from school despite their orders. Consequently my father, being their leader, was expelled!

He went into the hills of Cilicia and secretly organized Armenian language classes for children, who were totally ignorant of their mother tongue. It was there that Dr. A. H. Djebejian, a prominent physician in Aintab and member of the college's Board, found him. He brought him back to Aintab and convinced the school authorities to reinstate him.

Thus he was able to graduate. He did so in 1915; and soon after he was drafted into the Turkish army, where he and other Armenian soldiers were not allowed to bear arms. This was the policy for fear of insurrection by Armenian elements in the army. He was captured by the British forces, led by General Allenby, in the battle for Palestine, which culminated in the capture of Jerusalem in 1917. He was taken to Egypt as a prisoner of war. When they discovered his talent as a linguist and knowledge of English and Turkish, he was employed as the chief translator for General Allenby and his officers.

In the course of his service there, one day he was escorted into a tent where a high-ranking officer interrogated him about his knowledge of the terrain in eastern Turkey and Syria. He later realized that this officer was the famous Lawrence of Arabia, who had been plotting sorties of resistance and rallying the Arabs' rebellion against the Ottoman powers.

In 1918, with the conclusion of World War I, my father was granted his freedom, and he returned to Aintab. From there, the story gets somewhat fuzzy, but I remember hearing that he went to Adana (southern Cilicia) and worked in the YMCA there, teaching remnants of the Armenian Genocide, our language, and culture. Eventually he secured a temporary travel document, called "Laissez-Passer," from the French authorities who had taken charge of Cilicia, Turkey under a mandate from the League of Nations following the Great War. He travelled by ship from the port of Mersin, near Adana, to Cyprus, landing in Larnaca on November 22, 1921.

In Larnaca, where I was born in 1931, my father Manuel was employed as a teacher in the American Academy, an educational institution established in 1908 by the Mission Board of the Reformed Presbyterian Church of North America. He served them for forty years as librarian and as instructor of mathematics, geography, and the Armenian and Turkish languages. His biography is fully included in a 2005 book by Dr. Yervant Kassouny titled, *Manuel S. Kassouni, Historical Studies, Observations and Remembrances.* It is mostly in Armenian with several chapters in English.

My mother played no lesser a role in the formation of my identity. Martha Mississian was a graduate of the Central Turkey Girls College in Marash. She did not tell us this, but I gathered it from others who knew that she had been engaged to marry a man in Marash. However, in her full view, several Turks attacked and killed him in a street. I also picked up the story that a dashing Turkish officer had seen this beautiful young woman and sought to claim her as his wife. However, on hearing this she quickly prepared to flee and did so soon after. My uncle the Rev. Yeghia Kassouny, who was teaching in the Theological Seminary in Marash, got to know Martha and recommended to my father that he seek her as his wife. This he succeeded in doing, thank God.

We know very little of my mother's family or of her childhood home. She used to tell us about her sisters, whom we never met, except that many years later we did meet two of her nieces, Aznive Meykhanejian and Sirvart Yedikian and their respective families. She hardly ever talked to us about her early life. We do know, however, that her family came from a village not far from Marash called Zeitoun (meaning Olive in Turkish). This village was famous for its heroic resistance against Turkish incursions until the onset of genocide. Her mother brought her to the school when she was a young girl and entrusted her to the missionaries for her well-being and education. She absorbed their Christian and spiritual influence clearly and passed it on to us effectively.

She had a beautiful voice, rising early to sing carols at Christmas time and hymns at Easter to wake us with angelic messages. However, our neighbors did not appreciate it that much! We had a little pump organ in our home at which she gathered us and friends for times of joyful song-fest. Alas, rheumatoid arthritis took her gift away, and her gnarled hands and fingers silenced her forever. Martha had a keen mind and profound spiritual commitment and sensitivities. She was the one who insisted we have family devotions, with readings in the big family Bible every morning. I still have that family Bible among my prized possessions.

She had a vibrant tenacity that prevailed through thick and thin. Her fragile health was her greatest obstacle preventing her from a full enjoyment of life and accomplishing her dreams. She was chronically ill with one ailment or another, the most serious of them being rheumatoid arthritis. As a deacon in our church, she was quite ahead of her time in emphasizing and celebrating the place of women in the band of Jesus's followers. Among many other duties she assumed, one was baking the unleavened bread for the sacrament of communion in our church. She also organized the six of us (father, mother, and four children) into a Kassouni Family Sextet. We sang mostly in church. I like to think we were the Armenian version of the von Trapp Family Singers, made famous by the movie *The Sound of Music!*

I was the youngest in a family of four children including two sisters, Nouvart and Agnes, and a brother, Sarkis. The Great Depression and World-War-II years were formative for us in many ways. A joy-filled home lived in frugality and scarcity taught us that material things were not the secret of happiness. We were wealthy in terms of values, intellectual pursuits, education, and social and spiritual relationships and friendships, in a neighborhood that included a number of families close to us.

Our small local church, the Bible, and the hymnbook were the source of spirituality, foundational in terms of our identity as Armenian evangelicals/Protestants. I loved the hymns we sang. From time to time,

I used to take our hymnbook to the roof top of our house in the village of Lefkara, where we moved for two years during the War, and sang every hymn I knew, starting from the first page to the last. The clue to my pursuing the pastoral ministry as a vocation dates back to when as a little boy I sat in the front row in church, along with all the other children, and absorbed much that had nothing to do with the sermon. It was preached in Turkish, which our parents understood but not we. What I absorbed had a lot to do with the atmosphere created by the congregation, the singing, the praying, and the listening.

I used to gaze on the pastor with deep fascination, awe, and imagination. He was the Rev. Youhanna Mugar. He was a tall man with a commanding figure. He used to preach with grand dramatic gestures. He had a high forehead with a receding hairline, which somehow captured my attention. One day, when he was visiting our home, after staring at him for a few minutes, I went to the bedroom, and taking a pair of scissors, I cut off the hair on the front of my head. Then I proudly walked back to the living room!

Aghast at the sight, my mother exclaimed, "What did you do to your hair?"

"I cut it so I could look like our pastor," I replied.

"I want to be like him some day!" Fortunately, I still have my hair to this day.

As Armenians, our identity has had much by way of ups and downs, points and counterpoints, imponderables and paradoxes. As Protestants, we were accused of not being "real" Armenians by the community at large. They called us "*Porod*," which is a takeoff on the word "Protestant." However, the word in Armenian means "leper!" Again, my inspiration in that regard was my father who proudly practiced his faith in our Protestant/Evangelical community and also mingled and participated in the worship and life of the Armenian Apostolic church as well. There he trained their church choir, where my sister Nouvart also sang. He formed a society for the preservation and promotion of the Armenian language and culture, and he gathered young men around him at the sea-front Armenian Club. He talked about our history and our national identity with them, while he squeezed in a game or two of backgammon and sipped a hot cup of Turkish coffee. His love of the board game extended all the way to our house where the local Armenian priest used to come to visit us. The two would sit down to a loud game of backgammon on our front porch, to the consternation of my mother who used to caution dad, saying, "Quiet, the neighbors will hear you!"

My father was a student and a scholar who was an authority on Armenian history and the whole Middle East. He lectured often and was the author of many articles. He had an admirable counterpoint to the points of accusation directed at us. He stood tall and never acted out of a sense of inferiority because we did not belong to the mainstream of Armenian Apostolic (Orthodox) religious and national identity. He passed that on to us, including me, as a priceless gift indeed.

Early in our life we became aware of and struggled with the fact that the American mission in Cyprus, which was established and maintained by the Reformed Presbyterian Church in America, had worship practices which were contrary and restrictive for us Armenians who came from Turkey. There our people were Congregationalists, following the faith and practices taught to them by their mentors, missionaries of the American Board of Commissioners for Foreign Missions. Hearty singing of hymns accompanied by piano and other musical instruments was promoted and practiced with much enthusiasm in our homes.

However, due to the fact that there was no other Protestant church in Larnaca, our people opted to affiliate with the Reformed Presbyterian Church (called the RP Church). They held to a strict order of worship that used the Psalms exclusively in singing the faith and allowed no type of musical instrument whatsoever as accompaniment.

Constant debates, arguments, and ill feeling hounded us for years in this regard. Again, my father pointed us in the right direction. As a ruling elder, lay preacher, and Bible teacher, he led us to be supportive members of the RPC. He translated the Psalter (the Psalms with music) into Armenian and published a unique book, which we used for years in our services. I treasure both his personal copy of the English version of *The Book of Psalms with Music*, dated November 28, 1929, and also the Armenian version which he authored and printed with a small printing press he owned and operated in those years, dating back to the year 1931, the year of my birth. It contains all 150 Psalms in Armenian and thirty-four in the Turkish language.

This little church was our spiritual home. I was baptized there, received my early education in the Bible and the Gospel there, and participated in a community of great love and support; and it launched me into the world, like a ship going out to sea.

The American Academy of Larnaca, Cyprus has been an amazing educational institution, still going strong today, albeit free from the RPC and American missionaries' control. My father was a teacher and librarian there for forty years, and all our education was free of charge. Teaching us to speak, think, and write in English was the Academy's forte. However, the grand result was that it oriented us to look westward to America for our destiny, spiritual and physical. We were taught English and American history, but not our own. This compounded my sense of alienation from citizens of Cyprus and my own Armenian people and directed me to America, where I did actually land in 1949, the year of my graduation from the Academy.

The point is that we flourished in every sense because of our spiritual and educational training. I am profoundly grateful for this legacy, and my whole ministerial career is based on that. However, the counterpoint is that I turned my face to the West, to America, and my back on our own national heritage for many years, until by a conscious resolve on my part I returned to the Armenian people, pastored their churches, and celebrated their story.

The whole Middle East has been under the sway of colonialism for over two hundred years. Now, we are experiencing its decline and passing, paralleling the dominance and decline of Western (European/American) powers there. Churches; schools and universities; hospitals; and centers for the caring of the blind, the poor, and the disabled have either ceased to exist or have been transferred to local indigenous constituencies. This phenomenon reflects the political realignment of states in the Middle East moving further and further from being pro-Western, and more and more independent or anti-Western. This is mostly due to the never-ending crises in regard to Israel, its unconditional support by America, and Palestinians seeking their independent nation in the West Bank. From here resentment and alienation have spread to most of the other nations in the Middle East. This situation is the incubator that has created explosive radical Islam and fierce reaction to Western culture and religions in the Middle East.

By way of counterpoint to this decline of the old American missionary-controlled institutions, we now have a new flow of Christian evangelical mission enterprises emerging in the Middle East. Their aggressive evangelism and promotion of the Gospel are making a noteworthy impression. It remains to be seen what their lasting impact will be. They are not afraid to address Muslims with the Gospel, and they use multimedia communications to spread it. The new churches that they are establishing include converts from Islam.

To my great surprise, for example, I hear that in Turkey there are now fledgling young churches started and maintained by Turkish converts to Christ. Several years ago, while attending the Convention of Christian Aid Mission (Bob Finley's organization) in Niagara Falls, Canada, I actually met a young Turkish Christian who was in the process of growing one such church back home in Turkey. I have talked to some of our Armenian pastors who have gone to Turkey and worshipped with them. I hear there are Turkish converts who meet for worship even in our Gedig Pasha Armenian Evangelical Church in Istanbul. There, they witnessed services when, with tears in their eyes, the Turkish brethren have asked for forgiveness for the horrible events of the Armenian Genocide. How about that!

Life During World War II

World War II came and went, leaving its indelible mark on Cyprus, as it did throughout the whole world. However, we were very fortunate in that there was no invasion, even though we dug air-raid shelters and often ran into them when the sirens blew. I was only eight years old in 1939 when Britain, whose colony we were at the time, declared war against Germany and its allies on September 3.

That evening, the elders of our church came to our home for a somber consultation. My father was the highly respected leader among them. He was calm, collected, and very measured in his approach to the crisis. He displayed a temperament and spirit that were inspirational for me. His calmness spread to us all. Henceforth, all I had to do in the many crises we faced was to look at him and believe that all would be fine. He often used the expression "God is great" to assure us that we were under God's sovereign care. How ironic that this expression is the rallying cry of Islam, "Allahu Akbar!" Somehow, when it is said in Armenian, it does not sound as ominous as when it is said in Arabic. I suppose one reason for that is that for us it is an expression of caring love and providence, whereas for Islam, along with their daily lives, it is their battle cry of war.

Allied troops were stationed in Cyprus as armies gathered for war. They were stationed in buildings around our town, and before long our school buildings were taken over by the government as barracks for their use. Among these were British, French, Australian, New Zealander, and Indian troops. When France surrendered to Germany in 1942, the French troops were assembled on our soccer field. Two flags went up: one for Free France and the other for Vichy France. We watched as the soldiers were called to stand under the flag they chose. Subsequently they were shipped either to join General Charles De Gaulle and the Resistance or to occupied Vichy France.

Hanging around army camps was for us youth a fascinating time indeed. We watched Indians bake their thin chapatti bread on open fires and chat in unknown tongues. We watched with fascination the Gurkhas and the famous knives they always wore at their side. We were told that they never took the knife out of its sheath and then never replaced it without first drawing blood, whether it be the enemy's, or if not, their own. We were happy that they were on our side in this war! Sikhs with their turbans and beards were another group that drew our interest.

What impressed me the most, however, was their skill at playing field hockey, which is a sport I played on our school team in high school. They were fast, sleek, and sharp, seldom losing to opposing teams. Boys hanging around army camps tend to pick up unsavory language, as was the case with me. I picked up words I did not understand, and then I mimicked the soldiers at home, trying to impress everyone. My brother, six years older than I, knew their meaning. He would try to shut me up, cautioning me that such language was bad. I would then run to mother and seek her support. My poor mother, who had no idea what the words meant, would say to Sarkis, "Let Vartkes alone, and don't interfere!" Poor Sarkis!

In 1941, soon after the government requisitioned our school, we were told that the Academy was being moved to the village of Lefkara, over twenty miles away in the hills, where it would be housed in a school building there. My father, being a teacher, decided to make the move also, and he rented our house to the government. Indian soldiers were housed there, and when we returned after two years, the place was a mess. The basement ceiling was black with soot because they used it to bake their bread on open fires on the concrete floor.

For me, two years in Lefkara were exciting years. We took up residence in the center of town. Our house had a flat roof which I used for my boyhood reveries and for viewing over rooftops, the neighborhood, and the countryside. It was my magic castle! This was my first experience away from home, in a village made famous by its lace called "*Lefkaritiko.*" Women dressed in black used to sit for hours in narrow alleys outside their homes, quietly and expertly making lace. Their husbands would take the finished product in suitcases to foreign countries to sell. Many homes today are graced with this fine handwork, and we are told that even the famous Cathedral in Milan has a priceless piece on its altar. That art is slowly going extinct because fewer and fewer women are making lace by hand, and handmade lace is being replaced by cheap and plentiful machine-made imitations.

Expansion of knowledge, consciousness, and fascination with na-ture were integral parts of my life in those early, preadolescent years. Several families, including ours, went on a picnic one day. We walked a mile or two into the hills and settled along a fascinating stream, full of sights and sounds new to me. I had never seen one before, except in picture books. Larnaca had no flowing streams, only dry gullies that filled with water for an hour or less during the few rainstorms that came our way.

"Where is all this water coming from?" I wondered, since it was not raining. My curiosity took charge, and I began to walk upstream with the idea that just around the next bend I would discover its source. However, as the sun began to sink low, I had enough brains to go back to the group even though I hadn't discovered the answer to my inquiry. Reluctantly I returned before it got dark and was quickly surrounded by anxious parents and friends saying excitedly, "Where have you been? We thought you were lost and were beginning to panic!" Needless to say, I learned something precious about my place in a loving and caring community that day.

Our community included twenty to twenty-five families of Armenians in its inner circle and a number of school- related teachers and mission-aries in the outer circle. We lived close to each other and spent much time in each other's homes, as if they were our own. That was our "village that raised the child" (as Hillary Clinton emphasized so eloquently). We were looked down upon by the native Greeks as being foreigners. There were times when open conflict and fights broke out between them and us. We used to make our own kites and fly them in the open fields. Once, when I was flying my kite, several Greek boys came and stood around watching. Suddenly, one of them pulled out a knife and cut the line of the kite. All we could do was race to catch the kite now flying free. We caught it several blocks away, entangled in a tree. And so it went for us growing up in a fascinating community with different nationalities thrown together.

Ironically, native Turks had a common language with our people, who were mainly Turkish speaking, and thus we did not encounter open hostility from them. Our church services, especially the sermons, were in the Turkish language. This created a big problem for the youth who were born in Cyprus and had no desire to perpetuate the use of that tongue. Eventually an agreement was reached, and our pastor was allowed to preach one sermon a month in Armenian.

Our house had no electricity and only one faucet in the kitchen for running water. Hence, hand-lit kerosene lanterns were our source of light. However, Sarkis Agha Gulesserian, a prominent man in our "village," was a clothing merchant, who always had a horse-drawn carriage take him to the family's shop. As it took off, we used to hitch a ride in the back, on a bar connecting the two wheels. His wife, Mrs. Elleni, liked me very much and always pinched my cheek in affection when she hugged me. She had a generous heart, and she sometimes played a joke on me. Because we did not have electricity, and they did, she used to give me burned-out bulbs to play with. I used to take them home, string them up to the ceiling, and ask my parents in frustration why they did not light up, as they did in the Gulesserian house! Obviously, my upbringing was in the prescientific era, what I now call "our Stone Age."

Our house and the Gulesserian house were the two houses that played significant roles in my growth and identity. Among the many reasons that I could recite for this fact, this one stands out: two works of art, one in their house and one in ours. In our living room hung a framed copy of *Hope*, by George Frederic Watts (nineteenth century). I had lost the name and author of this work till I was startled to read about it in Martin Luther King's book, *Strength to Love* (Fortress Press Philadelphia, 1985). It depicted a lone and forlorn and blindfolded woman sitting atop the world, holding a harp and plucking only one string, all the others having been broken. My mother must have hung it there for the times from which they had come (the Genocide years) and the times in which we found ourselves, the bleak and scary years of World War II. I used to stand there for long periods, gazing up at her, thinking "play on" and "believe." Many times in those terrible years, when all we had was "one string" to play on, we did just that! By God's grace that one last string never did break, because we never stopped believing and we never gave up hope. While researching this piece of art (by Google), I came upon the very exciting fact that it was President Barack Obama's favorite art-piece, and that his famous declaration of the "audacity of hope" is based on it. He had heard his pastor the Rev. Dr. Wright in Chicago preach, using this piece of art as his illustration; and he coined the term "audacity of hope." I also have discovered that Nelson Mandela, in his years of incarceration and torture, also used it for his inspiration. It is noteworthy to me that all these were from a persecuted, oppressed, and struggling people; and it is certainly understandable why they would look to it as a source of courage, resistance, and hope.

The other piece of art was that of Kramer Franz (1840–1900). It is based on the event in the wilderness of Sinai when Moses was instructed to make a bronze serpent, nail it to a pole, lift it high, and call on people bitten by snakes to look up and be healed. It has been used as a meta-phor for Christ on the Cross, "Just as Moses lifted up the serpent in the wilderness, so must the Son of Man be lifted up, that whoever believes in him may have eternal life" (John 2:14,15).

Franz Kramer's large painting hung in the foyer of the Gulesserian house in all its colorful, powerful, commanding, and mesmerizing pull on the viewer, me! It depicted people devastated by snake bites and in the final throes of life. In their midst stood Moses holding high the pole, waiting. I used to plead with the fallen, "Just look up please! It will take only a second." However, they remained frozen in their positions of res-ignation and death. That scene captured my imagination and has settled into my brain, indelibly fixed there, like a Mount Rushmore.

Fimie Gulesserian, one of their daughters, was the musician in that family. Among her many gifts, were her beauty (pink cheeks and blue eyes) and a gracious spirit. She played the piano (they had a shiny black upright, with brass candleholders on each side) and was also our youth choir leader. Around ten of us would gather around the piano and follow instructions. There was a problem, however, in that one of our group members, Hovsep Arabajian, could not carry a tune at all. Poor Fimie, she tried and tried but could not get a tune out of him. He was one of us, however, and we would not let her dismiss him; so that possibility was rejected. Well, she finally settled on one. "You stand in the back row, and just open and close your mouth and pretend you are singing. But don't let any noise come out!" Well, it did not quite work that well, but we loved Hovsep, and he "sang" on with us anyway.

The Second World War had its many points and influences that helped shape my life. Germany did not invade our island, even though we were in great fear that after the capturing of Crete and the fall of Greece in 1941, when hordes of paratroopers rained down from the sky, we would be next. The Germans pushed across North Africa and arrived at the gates of the Suez Canal in Egypt. The great battle of El Alamein in 1942 was the turning point, to our great relief. Field Marshal Montgomery led the Allies in a historic battle that stopped the legendary Rommel from capturing Suez and turned the German armies back westward in retreat. We were certain that if the Germans took Egypt, we would surely be invaded and overrun next. All the horrible consequences accompanying occupation constantly played in our minds as a real possibility.

We built an air-raid shelter in the yard of our neighbors, the Baltayans. Our trusty old wooden ladder went into supporting the roof over a simple trench, covered with pieces of wood and mud, and that was essentially it. The air-raid sirens would sound, and both families would scamper into it. However, we, the boys, would not sit still. We would run outside and watch to see if we could catch a glimpse of the attacking planes. By the sound of their engines we could tell if they were German or Italian. If Italian (with a steady sound), we would not worry because their bombs seldom hit anything important. Actually, the joke was that they helped the people by feeding them with the fish killed when they dumped their bombs in the sea and hurried back to their bases! The German planes, however, had an undulating rhythm in their engines, and when we recognized them we would run back into the shelter, because they could do serious damage. In one such raid, a woman in our church family was killed when her house was bombed. It was a mistaken target, for nearby was a park with hidden fuel tanks for the military. Pieces of shrapnel from bombs became paper weights cherished as mementos, another example of life's ironies during war time.

Following their retreat from Egypt, a number of German prisoners of war were brought to Cyprus to be held there till the war ended. One of their camps was in Dikkelia, about eight miles east of Larnaca, where the British had a big military base. Among the prisoners were a number of Protestants. Our missionary leaders Dr. Wilbur W. Weir and his wife Elizabeth, who was our youth group leader, announced that the prisoners of war, accompanied by their chaplain, would like to come to our church services, if we had no objection. We were assured that they would sit in a separate section of the sanctuary and have no interaction with us. So it was that for several weeks, we had this strange and yet very meaningful experience of enemies in war coming together to worship God, brought there by the Gospel of Jesus Christ.

Mrs. Weir was the link between us; and after the war ended, she kept up correspondence between the chaplain and us. She informed us that there was much hunger and destitution in Germany and invited us to help them out. So we proceeded to prepare care packages of canned food, nuts, dried food, beans, and grains and mail them to the chaplain for distribution among his people.

Participating in this effort had a profound influence on me; I marvel that we were able to do all that without rejecting them. Christ said, "Love your enemies." This was a powerful truth brought home to me. St. John also said, "Perfect love casts out fear." Thus a very powerful demonstration of life's paradoxes was made for me in my impressionable years, as I sought to form an understanding of what it meant to be a Christian.

Our only source for news concerning the progress of the war was the local newspaper, the *Cyprus Mail.* We had no radio in our home then. The paper became for me my geography and history book. By carefully following the daily news and maps, I learned a lot about North Africa, Italy, Western and Eastern Europe, and the Far East. I learned about countries, cities, rivers, mountains, peoples, and their governments. Our fate was in the hands of their leaders. Aligned against the Axis powers of Adolph Hitler (Germany) and Benito Mussolini (Italy) were the Allied powers, led by Winston Churchill (Great Britain), Joseph Stalin (Soviet Union), and Franklin Roosevelt (USA), and their increasingly invincible armies, navies, and air forces.

My brother Sarkis, who was six years my senior, and his friend Kevork Kevorkian went missing in 1944. My parents were beside themselves wondering what had happened to them. They were gone with no note or message left behind with anyone. Fears of foul play were paramount in our thinking. Several days later the mystery was solved. They had run away and joined the British Navy, which had whisked them away to Egypt! Great was our relief, but anxiety persisted because of possible injury or death in some battle somewhere unknown to us. However, we began receiving reports that they were in the desert town of Ismailia in southern Egypt, working to maintain supplies to our troops. At the end of the war, they returned hale and hearty with stories not of bravery in war but of their shenanigans and exploits with the natives.

My sister, Nouvart, eight years my senior, went to Beirut, Lebanon, in 1942 to attend BSTC (British Syrian Training College) and receive training to be a teacher. The big hole left in our family was deeply painful, especially for my mother. She cried daily and pined for her daughter, not knowing how she'd fare while there. Our beloved pet dog, Rover, Nouvart's darling, felt her absence very keenly also. Alas, one winter morning we found that he had crept under her bed and died. We were convinced he died of a broken heart.

Nouvart wrote to us of her progress as a student and as a teacher/ aide in an extremely rich Maronite home with hitherto unheard of luxuries and wealth. While in Beirut she was under the watchful eye of our uncle, the Rev. Yeghia and Mrs. Kassouny and family. Nouvart averted near disaster when she broke a surreptitiously arranged engagement with a Syrian/Armenian dentist. She courageously withstood all attempts to make her change her mind. She returned to Cyprus after her graduation and ended up marrying her high-school sweetheart, Hercules Panayiotides. He was the son of a dear couple in our local church, the Rev. Theodore and Mrs. Vasiliki Panayiotides.

Our heroes in those years were not movie stars but generals and field marshals leading the charge against the forces of the Axis powers. Names like Montgomery, Eisenhower, McArthur, and Patton were held in awe. We prayed for victory, and we cheered over every bit of news bringing hope of eventual triumph. It finally came on May 8, 1945 (V-E, or Victory in Europe day). I was fourteen by then. Adolescence had arrived for me. With a world now at peace and new opportunities and vistas opening up before us all, I was full of anticipation and dreams of a bright future. However, I still had a mountain to climb—four years of high school!

My Parents

My Mother, Martha Mississian

1. At age eight.
2. *Seated on right* with three other students and Miss Blakely, missionary/teacher *(seated at center)*. Central Turkey Girls College, Marash, Turkey, ca. 1918.
3. *Second from the right* with house parents *(seated)*. Marash, Turkey, ca. 1914.

My Father, Manuel Kassouni

4. A soldier in World War I with the British Army. Egypt, ca. 1918.
5. With his graduating class *(seated at center wearing white trousers)*. American Academy, Larnaca, Cyprus, ca. 1921.
6. With his brother, the Rev. Yeghia Kassouny. Aintab (modern-day Gaziantep), ca. 1914.

My Family

1. Manuel and Martha Kassouni wedding photo, May 20, 1922.
2. Manuel and Martha Kassouni, 1945.
3. Baby Vartkes, 1931.
4. My first family photo, ca. 1933. *Back, left to right*, father Manuel, brother Sarkis, sister Nouvart, sister Agnes, and mother Martha. *Front center*, me.
5. My sister Agnes and me, ca. 1938.

My Home

Map of Cyprus.Courtesy of http://ontheworldmap.com/cyprus/.

The house where I was born. Larnaca, Cyprus.

My home church where I was baptized. Larnaca, Cyprus.

Two

Transitions

From Childhood to Adolescence

The phenomenon of change is central to life. Usually, transitions are slow and normal. However, for us, in the mid-1940s, they were fast and unexpected. Change from childhood to adolescence was for me somewhat turbulent. Parents and siblings were not of much help. By the time my mother, with much hesitation and embarrassment, talked to me about "the birds and the bees," I had already discovered where babies came from. My father never said a word about this subject to me. Actually, when a school friend, years before in Lefkara, first told me how a woman became pregnant and bore a baby, I thought he was crazy!

"So how do you think it happens?" he asked.

"Just like a fruit tree. At a certain age, it starts bearing fruit, and so does a woman begin to have babies at a certain age," I replied.

How about that! Obviously, I did not know anything about pollination either.

Discovering and dealing with my own sexuality was a lonely journey for me, for I was left to figure things out as best as I could. My sources of information were contradictory and confusing. I bounced between a world of imagination and fantasy, vividly promoted by Hollywood movies, and the real world of strict religious taboos and values. We talked with girls at school, in church, and the neighborhood, but nothing more. We were not allowed to date, dance, or go to parties with girls in attendance. On Valentine's Day, the girls in our high school used to have a party just among themselves, properly supervised of course. And we boys, filled with curiosity as to what they were doing, would peek through the slats of the classroom windows to find out the answer to the mystery.

Friends, during my adolescent years, were my companions with whom I spent most of my time after school hours and weekends. We created our own games and roamed the fields behind our houses with no fear. We played soccer in our street and school yard. We went swimming in the summer, our favorite place being an old pier that was no longer used for commercial purposes. We would bring a small watermelon along and use it like a ball in the water. Ultimately, we would cut it and proceed to enjoy our delicious snack.

Three of us who were especially close were called "The Three Musketeers" (apologies to Alexander Dumas): they were Karnig Berberian, Hovsep Kehyaian, and myself. After our graduation from high school, we went our different ways. Karnig went to England, and I did not see him again till a few years ago when he moved to the United States. Sadly, the intensity of our friendship had cooled, and we were no longer that close. He passed away two years ago. His sister Zarouhi and my sister Agnes came to America together. His brother David, along with his wife Glissey, and I have become close friends, maintaining correspondence over these many years. They reside in Dallas, Texas. Every so often we meet and share our stories and our family news, and we reminisce about the good old days.

The transition from a war to a peacetime economy and life brought welcome changes to our home. After years of no electricity, we finally got wired for power, and the lights came on. No more lighting kerosene lamps and hanging them on the walls at night. We had a new bathroom with running water and a hot-water heater for our showers now. No more a hole in the floor. It was a great event in our house when a flush toilet was installed. I enjoyed pulling the chain and seeing the water run down from the tank overhead.

We finally had our own radio also. It was a Phillips short-wave radio, and we used to sit around it every evening listening to the news about what was going on in the rest of the world. We were no longer isolated. The world was beginning to open up to me, and my imagination about it began to soar.

Contributing a tremendous and inordinate amount to my fantasy life, developing in my mind now with great speed, was the world of Hollywood. I used to save every penny, beg and borrow from parents and friends, and then run to the movies. Sunday afternoons, as soon as we got out of our youth Christian Endeavor meeting, we rushed downtown to the cinema to catch the latest movie. One ingenious way we got in for free was taking the hand of an acquaintance just as he was to enter, and go in as his guest, since children accompanied by adults were allowed in for free.

Scouting and sports were the passion of my life. I could not wait to arrive at the age when I could join the Boy Scouts. I used to envy my older brother, who was a Scout and having a ball with friends going on camping trips and hanging out with them all the time. When I finally was able to join, I took to it like a fish to water. I rose in the ranks until I was chosen to be the Scoutmaster of the Armenian elementary school in our town. We had some intriguing experiences in scouting. When trying to pass my Tenderfoot class exam, my teacher, Mr. Aram Tchaderjian, asked me to fry two eggs on an open campfire. In the process of doing so, one egg yolk broke. To my utter amazement, he reprimanded me.

"You fail because you broke the yolk," he said.

"But it is a perfectly good egg!" I replied.

"Sorry, you have failed," he insisted.

"Well, I'll eat it myself then," I responded and proceeded to have my breakfast alone. Nevertheless, I had to try again later, and I made sure the yolks were not broken then.

On another occasion, we went on a camping day trip to woods a mile or two outside our town. At lunchtime, we were told to eat anything we had brought along. Well, my friend Sedat Aktay (he was Turkish, by the way) and I had brought nothing edible, so we decided to walk among the trees and hunt for birds with our slings. We succeeded in shooting a bird, and we proceeded to roast it on an open fire. With great pride in our hunting prowess, we took one leg of the roasted bird and brought it to our scoutmaster, George Moissides, as a gift to share our lunch. To our utter surprise, he was aghast at what we had done, and to our great disappointment, he accused us of being cruel to animals and breaking one of the Scout laws. He was not satisfied to leave it at that and called the troop to a court martial gathering a few days later. Dressed in full scouting regalia, we were called forward to respond to the charge laid against us. I told Sedat to let me speak first in our defense.

"Mr. Moissides, are you a vegetarian?" I asked.

"No," he replied.

"In that case, sir, I assume you eat beef?"

"Yes, I do."

"Well," I responded, "the cow had to be slaughtered for the sake of providing meat, and we shot the bird to have our lunch. What is the difference? We did not torture the bird. We killed it for food!"

We won the case unanimously and were cleared of breaking the Scout laws.

Scouting was a family passion, including my brother Sarkis and my sisters Nouvart and Agnes. Nouvart was one of the highest-ranked Girl Guide (named so in the British Empire, but Scout in America) leaders in Cyprus. That worked to her advantage because when Princess Elizabeth (later crowned Queen) got married to Prince Philip in 1947, she was the head of all the Girl Guides in the British Empire. Consequently, pieces of her wedding cake were sent to all the colonies, to be distributed among the leaders. Cyprus being among them, Nouvart eventually got her share as well. She gathered all six of us in the family around the dining room table and with great care unwrapped the cake. It was well preserved, being a fruit cake, and her share was about two inches long, one inch wide, and half an inch thick. She ceremoniously cut it into six pieces, and she extended to each one of us our share. I have often referred to that great event as the time I was inducted into British royalty!

Sports were a great passion for me, to the point that my studies suffered and I had to repeat ninth grade. After that scary experience and a good talk with my father, I settled down, and my last three years were academically very good. We played soccer every chance we had, often till the sun set. Real soccer balls were expensive and hard to get, so we played with old tennis balls instead. That was a very good way to learn ball control, however. The greatest Christmas gift I ever received as a young boy was a new soccer ball.

We hung around the tennis courts of the school and became ball boys for a few shillings. We took up discarded rackets because we could not afford to buy new ones; we hand strung them with pliers and started playing tennis at around age fourteen. I was able to develop my skills, and all my life I have continued to play.

In my senior year, 1949, I reached the school tennis-championship match. To my dismay, however, I needed a new pair of tennis shoes desperately if I was to compete effectively. Having hardly any money, I rushed downtown and bought a cheap pair for one pound (around three dollars). Then I rushed back and arrived in time to play. After only a few minutes, the shoes split, and I was left in utter dismay. Give it up now, or play on with split-open shoes. Well, I proceeded to play anyway and finished a very poor second.

I played field hockey on our American Academy high school team, as well as basketball and volleyball. Our coach was Giragos Chopourian, who went on to be ordained to the Christian ministry and eventually became the Executive Director of the Armenian Missionary Association of America. His greatest challenge as my hockey coach was to teach me to hold the stick properly, because I always placed my left wrist under my right wrist. Alas, it never worked, and he always reminded me of that the rest of my life when we served together in America as colleagues in ministry.

From Sleep to Awakening

Youth for Christ, an evangelical movement, arrived in Cyprus with a big bang in 1948. Our pastor, the Rev. Hagop Sagherian, had gone to Beatenberg, Switzerland to attend their international convention and caught the fire and vision for the evangelization of youth. While there, he met a dynamic evangelist, Robert Finley and a Filipino colleague of his, Greg Tingson. He invited them to come to Cyprus for an evangelistic crusade.

"Bob" Finley was a former US collegiate boxing champion at the University of Virginia, Charlottesville. He was a friend of Billy Graham's and preached in a similar style. He spoke in our school and in our church and began to create quite a stir among us. He came to our tennis court one morning and asked to play with us. We were flattered that he would want to do so but soon found out that he was not a good tennis player. He approached me after a while and asked if he could have a talk with me. I was more than happy to say yes. An American celebrity wishing to talk to me! Wow! In the course of our conversation about this and that, he asked me a searching question that went right to my heart: "Vartkes," he said. "Does Jesus Christ have any place in all the hopes and dreams that you have for your life?"

I already believed in Jesus Christ and had joined our church as a communicant member three years before. His question was not one of intellectual belief, which I had, but one of commitment, which I did not have. I proceeded to say that, in all honesty, I had no such commitment. My hopes and dreams were of moving away from Cyprus, of discovering the new world we had just inherited after the war, and of finding education and success in a career of some sort. He followed his question with a very persuasive and moving challenge to me: to give my life (what that meant I was not sure) and to dedicate myself to the service of Jesus Christ.

"You can't have a more exciting and challenging life than that!" he stressed over and over. I was deeply moved, and I went home pondering this matter in the depths of my soul.

There was something different about the way Bob Finley approached me and engaged me in a deep conversation. I found out later that our principal, Mr. Wilbur Weir, and our pastor had told him I was the one to "win" and that the influence on my friends would be profound thereafter. Though I was a Christian, I had never been approached personally about the claims of Jesus Christ on my life by any pastor, evangelist, teacher, or parent. I had heard many sermons and appeals to "receive Christ as my Savior and Lord," and I thought I had done that, but this was different. That night, I tossed and turned in my bed and struggled with the answer. Yes or no? Commitment and a turnaround in the direction that my life was to take, or continuation of life as usual and maintaining a nominal Christian identity through it all.

My struggle was two-fold: first, a full-hearted commitment to Christ on the one hand. Secondly, a commitment to the service of Christ in a Christian vocation, such as ordained ministry, evangelist, or missionary. I was struggling with his original question put to me. What place *did* Christ now have in my plans and dreams for my life's direction?

My struggle came to a climax sometime in the middle of the night. I got up, knelt at my bedside, and in a prayer of confession and commitment, said "Yes!" to Christ. I pledged myself to him and to his service as the only viable option for my future.

The next day I sought out Mr. Finley and told him what had transpired the night before. I also told him that I had made a profoundly important decision concerning my future, which was full-time ministry in the service of Christ, whether here in Cyprus, in the Middle East, or wherever that may be. I added that since I was only a year away from graduation, I would want to find a college where my training for ministry could begin. Needless to say, he was overjoyed. Then he said,

"Next year, after your graduation, I give you my word that you will be enrolled in a Christian College, and I will help you with scholarship aid. So begin to make your preparations accordingly."

Wow! That was something straight out of heaven for me! Things moved fast from then on. The news got out, and our youth-group meeting was packed the next Sunday evening when I shared my testimony and called on my friends to also make their commitment. That coming week a Youth for Christ rally was held in the local cinema hall. This was a first for our town and curiosity brought at least two hundred people out to it. I was asked to share my testimony there, and I was scared to death. My knees were literally shaking as I sat on the platform waiting for my turn to speak. However, as soon as I stood up, a strange calm came over me, and I delivered my talk smoothly and clearly. That was the beginning of my public ministry in the cause of Christ, which has now lasted over sixty years.

I have pondered long and hard to understand my experience from a theological perspective. The term used in evangelical circles is that of "being born again," as per Jesus's conversation with Nicodemus recorded in the Gospel of John, chapter 3. How do I reconcile this event with the lifelong identity I had, beginning with my baptism, growing up in a loving Christ-centered home, and being a regular member of my church as a communicant? I have heard people with similar experience discount all that kind of background as being almost worthless until one is "born again." Well, I cannot downplay my past as being worthless in that regard. I feel it is essentially a process in which the grace of God took charge of my life and led me through step by step.

My present experience of spiritual awakening did not nullify my past experiences but affirmed them and completed my spiritual identity. From my birth, God's grace was at work without my conscious understanding or commitment. This experience of surrender of will to God in Christ freed me from internal turmoil and a double-minded approach to my life. I affirmed by personal choice what God's hand had already accomplished for me in Christ. My parents, my church, and my school, all had their part in this process, and the final climactic component was added by Bob Finley's personal work with me as an agent of Christ's Holy Spirit. They all had made their point. Now my personal decision provided the counterpoint. One did not cancel the other out but was complementary and positive.

When we take for granted that baptism and church membership are sufficient, we leave out that dimension of personal and conscious commitment necessary for Christian experience. This is a big reason why many of our young people leave our churches and join new evangelical churches. "What will you do with Jesus?" is a question calling one's total body and soul for a response. An evangelistic approach and witness are absolutely important. One must do it, however, in a very sensitive, loving, and nonmanipulative manner. For example, one wrong approach is using "hell-fire and damnation" imagery or language. I'd heard that kind of preaching many times before with decreasing effectiveness. "Eternal fire insurance" may be taken out by some, however, with dubious results, in terms of the claims of the Gospel. Christ's call and invitation are to life abundant now, on earth, while we are still living. That's what caught my attention with Bob Finley's approach to me. He used the central teaching of Jesus in talking to me. "I have come that they might have life, and have it more abundantly." That's it, pure and simple, and it has been my conviction and approach ever since.

That event in 1948 became a springboard for my life, catapulting me into fast-changing environments and experiences. As I began to set the stage for my life as a ministerial student after high school, Bob Finley played an increasingly central role in helping me move forward. He did not stay long in Cyprus, but he moved on to his mission in Asia, landing him in China in those turbulent years of civil war. He did not forget what he had promised me. He contacted Dr. Bob Jones Jr., president of Bob Jones University in Greenville, South Carolina and arranged for me to enroll there in the coming year.

"And how shall I finance my education?" was my concern. "My parents cannot in any way provide me with financial support, and I have no other resources."

Bob Finley's answer was in the form of a quotation from Paul's letter to the Philippians, 4:19: "My God will fully satisfy every need of yours according to his riches in glory in Christ Jesus." Preceding that verse was Paul's claim in verse 18: "I have been paid in full and have more than enough." This was his faith according to which he had embarked on a world mission of bringing Christ to the throngs of people he reached.

I was totally wrong in thinking that here was a "rich American" who would help to finance my trip to America and my education there. He taught me that the essential ingredient absolutely necessary to live the life of faith is utter dependency and trust in God's word and action in Christ. He himself was not dependent on any financial resources he had but on the loving support of people in America who prayed for him and maintained support as agents of Christ. He was for me a living demonstration of Paul's words in the earlier section of Philippians 4:11–14, "I have learned to be content with whatever I have. I know what it is to have little, and I know what it is to have plenty. In any and all circumstances I have learned the secret of being well-fed and of going hungry, of having plenty and of being in need, I can do all things through him who strengthens me." I took this to heart and lived by it literally, as the days progressed and my time for my journey away from Cyprus approached.

Having gained a central motivation for my life and a focus on my future, I breezed through my senior year in high school with no academic difficulty. I applied to Bob Jones University and was accepted as a student, and I also was awarded a modest sum by way of scholarship aid. Most important of all, the university agreed to be my financial guarantor in regard to the US immigration authorities, so that I would not apply for public aid any time I was in that country. A "guarantor" was absolutely necessary for any foreign student entering America, and I would find out later just how true this was.

I got my passport and secured a visa for entry into the United States. However, there was one catch to that. Since the US embassy in Cyprus was not a consulate, it did not have the authority to issue visas. The embassy did all the paperwork and certified that I had fulfilled all the requirements and then instructed me that if I stopped on the way in Naples, Italy, there was a consulate there that would issue the actual visa. "A mere formality" I was told. Well, it turned out quite differently. The journey took almost three months, instead of two weeks. However, my experiences were quite formative in terms of my faith journey. I learned the meaning, by painful experience in Naples, of what Bob Finley had taught me from Philippians, chapter 4.

During my last year in Cyprus, before my departure to America, I immersed myself in the life and mission of our local church. Our Christian Endeavor youth group got very active in reaching out to the community with a witness for Christ. We began to make regular visits to patients in the hospital, which was across the street, and we embarked on an unusual project. We built a push cart with bicycle wheels, loaded it with Christian literature, pushed it down to the sea shore, roughly a mile away, and parked it at the cornice. There crowds would gather every evening to take in the salt air, enjoy some shish kebab, and visit with friends. We would ask Euclid Panayiotides, the older brother of Hercules, my brother-in-law, to make a short public address in Greek, and then we would invite those interested to linger and read the Gospel literature we had for them. Thus, we would share the Gospel personally with others and invite them to Christ's fellowship.

Our local church was under the jurisdiction of the Reformed Presbyterian Church, also known as the Covenanter Church. In my last year there, I did something to help the congregation along in developing and celebrating its own pastoral leadership with full authority to administer the sacraments, without always deferring to the missionary leaders. This was because our pastor, the Rev. Hagop Sagherian, was not ordained, and it did not seem like things were moving along so he could be. He was fully qualified, having graduated from the Near East School of Theology, and having served for several years already as our pastor. The problem was that he was not Reformed Presbyterian and their leader, the Rev. Clark Copeland, did not think he was ready to be ordained yet. He was waiting for Mr. Sagherian to accept their firm restriction on singing hymns and no instrumental music in worship, except the cappella singing of the Psalms. Consequently, it irked and pained me to see our pastor stand aside during baptisms and communions while the American missionary would take over.

The upshot of it is that my father helped me prepare a petition from the congregation calling on the Rev. C. Copeland to proceed to the ordination of our pastor, since he had fulfilled all other requirements. I took that petition personally to every member in our church, and they signed it with great encouragement. I then took it to Rev. Copeland and handed it to him. He was totally surprised and taken aback by it. He said that they would give it careful consideration. However, even after that, it took more than a year before Mr. Sagherian would be ordained. By then I had already left for America.

Our little church went through quite a struggle in seeking freedom to worship in accordance with our culture and beliefs, versus the dictates and beliefs of the Reformed Presbyterian Church. The issue was hymns and gospel songs accompanied by the piano, versus Psalms to be used in the worship services, which I had mentioned earlier.

Things came to a head with a formal letter, dated February 20, 1953, sent to the Board of Foreign Missions, Synod of the Reformed Presbyterian Church in North America. The letter was sent on behalf of the church's two branches, one in Nicosia and the other in Larnaca. It was signed by Samuel S. Mouradian, Apel Dombourian, and Nishan Helvadjian, elders of the Nicosia branch; and Sarkis Gulesserian and Manuel Kassouni, elders of the Larnaca branch. Rev. Hagop Sagherian, their Moderator, signed it as well.

I will quote extensively from this letter, a copy of which I've had in my possession these many years. It is a powerful and eloquent statement, a stand for freedom taken by believers appealing to a board, aptly called "of Foreign Missions" thousands of miles away. This letter is the last of a series of correspondences on the matter between the local church and the mission board in America. Here are significant excerpts:

Now that we have before us both your letter and Rev. Copeland's report we think it opportune to write to you after prayers and meditation on this subject. The experience of the last 30 years, together with our studies of the fundamental beliefs of the Covenanter Church of North America, have shown us that there is but one principal point concerning which the conviction and attitude of our Armenian churches differ from those of your church, namely, the manner of worship. Due to our historical background which we expressed somewhat in detail in our previous letter to you and some causative circumstances and events, the Armenian Evangelical Churches of Cyprus have not been convinced that in worship Psalms must exclusively be used without accompaniment of instrumental music.

But dear brethren, we want you to know and think it so, that ours is not, by any means, superstitiously and stubbornly sticking to some ancient sacred relic come to us from the church fathers, or sticking to some spiritual tradition left to us from our fathers. Ours is not superficial ambition of siding with the majority in the world. Ours is not to be arrogantly somebody different from you. But we want it to be known to you clearly that, we love singing hymns accompanied by instrumental music, because:

1. *Experimentally we have seen the great blessings of it in our own lives as individuals, as families, and as church groups.*
2. *We have seen the benefits of the great blessings of the gospel songs not only in our own lives but also in the lives of numberless dear children of God in the past and in the present.*

Beloved brethren, at the birth of our blessed Savior, the angels sang a divine hymn. In the book of Revelation we read that heaven was opened to the great apostle John who saw and heard...the four beasts and four and twenty elders fell down before the Lamb, having every one of them harps. And they sang a new song.

In an extraordinary congregational meeting in each church, *when your letter and Rev. Copeland's report were presented to the congregations, not one individual was found among those present who could conscientiously say that hymn singing in worship was wrong or sin. In the same congregational meeting the view was expressed that the Armenian churches do not cherish or favor the idea of separation, remembering well the fine and helpful Christian fellowship that we have had with you in the past 30 years.*

Concerning the particular matter between you and us, as expressed above, neither the two sessions nor the two congregations wish to be involved in further useless discussions, because the view and the convictions of both sides on the matter are quite clear and lucid. We believe in the use of Psalms and also gospel songs with accompaniment of instrumental music in worship. We believe with deep conviction that any song which is in line with the spirit and truth of the Word of God, which exalts the Lord Jesus, edifies the saints and helps the sinners to find the Savior is worthy to be used in worship.

We wish on this occasion to express our heartfelt gratitude and thanks to you for your Christian spirit which has enabled us to enjoy such fine fellowship with our missionary brethren in the past, now in the present, and we hope it will also be in the future.

This whole matter came to a conclusion with the release of the churches in question from the jurisdiction of the Synod. To this day they, and also their sister Greek Evangelical Church of Cyprus, which had similar conflicts, continue as independent ecclesiastical entities.

It is unfortunate, however, that at the time of writing of this book (2016), the Armenian Evangelical Church in Cyprus does not exist any longer due to the dispersion of the member families. There are less than a dozen Armenian Evangelical families left there. The Greek Evangelical Church, which inherited the historic church building in Larnaca, continues to meet there. My nephew, Hercules Jr., son of Hercules and Nouvart Kassouni Djaferis-Panayiotides, is an ordained minister and is serving in the Larnaca congregation as an elder.

From Local to Global

The year 1949 was a climactic year for me, as far as my life on Cyprus was concerned. It was a year of good-byes and preparation for the big journey ahead. I kept in constant touch with Bob Finley, my mentor and benefactor. From Cyprus he had moved on to India for several months, and then on to China. He was on his own, dependent completely on faith, and under no mission board of any kind. He was for me a living example of one who "lives by faith and not by sight" (St. Paul, in 2 Cor. 5:7).

At that time, China was going through a civil war and the turmoil that brought in the Communist regime. This necessitated his eventual departure (actually expulsion) from China. His utter dependence on God's providence took him through some trying times. He told me that when he was in India, he ran out of money, and the authorities were pressing him to leave the country, when he received a generous check from a farmer acquaintance back home in Charlottesville, Virginia. This dear man had been led by the Spirit to sell a cow and send the proceeds to Bob! Bob kept repeating his spiritual guiding light which he followed without hesitation: "My God shall supply all your need according to his riches in Christ Jesus" (Phil. 4:19). He sent me enough money to cover my passage to America and something extra for room and board in Naples, Italy, where I was to secure my visa to the United States because the Embassy in Cyprus was not yet authorized to do so.

Farewell parties at home, at church, and at school left me sad and yet excited that doors were opening for me on my faith and physical journey into the great world beyond. The excitement was accompanied by fears as well. I was eighteen years old and striking out by myself into the unknown! I was leaving behind my family, my friends, and my neighborhoods. The unlimited optimism and self-assurance of an eighteen-year-old, coupled with the faith that God was walking with me led me on.

In one of our gatherings to wish me well, my pastor, the Rev. Hagop Sagherian, said: "We are sending you to America as a missionary. That country is not all that you think it is. They need the Gospel, just as we do here." And my school principal, the Rev. Wilbur W. Weir said, "In America you will find the best of things and the worst of things. It is up to you to set the direction you will take. May God be with you." How well said by both these men of God. I never forgot their words and have discovered them to be absolutely true.

There were four of us who took off together for America, and all of us were scheduled to stop in Naples to secure proper visa papers from the American Embassy there. My sister Agnes and Zarouhi Berberian, who was from our church family, were registered to enter New York Bible Institute, in New York City, which changed its name some years later to become Sheldon College. The fourth was Euripides, a Cypriot Greek who was also a graduate of the American Academy. We boarded SS. Campidoglio at Larnaca on August 5, 1949, and arrived in Naples a week later. We proceeded immediately to the American Embassy, confident that we would be obtaining our papers with no trouble. However, we were deeply disappointed when we were informed that our papers were not in order. We needed adequate assurances from a financial guarantor in the United States that in the case of need we would not be dependent on public funds. My guarantor was Bob Jones University, Greenville, South Carolina, where I was headed. The school's papers of guarantee on my behalf were deemed inadequate because they did not reveal their actual financial assets. This became a sticking point over which the vice-consul, Mr. Lewis McCorquodale would not budge! When our dilemma was carefully considered, the other three decided to go back to Cyprus and try again when the US Embassy there would be qualified to issue visas. I was adamant in staying put, and my resolve was "God has led me thus far, and will lead me on from here. I do not backtrack!"

My stay in Naples stretched for several weeks and became a pivotal experience for me in many important ways. First, before the others left Naples, we looked for a Protestant church and finally found the local Methodist church, where we met two American missionaries working with Youth for Christ. Connecting with a local community of believers was central to our receiving support and encouragement. Next, my finances being extremely limited, I moved to a one-dollar-a-night flophouse in the harbor region of the city. I had only ninety dollars in my possession, and no other resource available.

I wrote to Dr. Bob Jones telling him what my dilemma was, assuring them that I would wait it out, and pleading with them to do something to move me out of the impasse. Every week when I received their response, saying in effect "Sorry, but we do not reveal our assets to anyone," I would then go to the embassy and hear all over again, "No, your papers are still not in order!" I'd lie on my bed in my dingy room and pray with the sound of departing ships in my ears, "God, why can't I be on one of those ships? Please help me to get through this dilemma!"

There, I began to understand that my calling to ministry would not be paved with rose petals and comfortable surroundings. God began to teach me how to suffer isolation, discomfort, and hunger, too, because I could not afford to go to restaurants for meals. Every morning I'd go to a bakery close by and get a loaf of fresh crunchy bread, and then I'd go to the grocer and buy a big bunch of grapes. That was it! I lived on bread and grapes for two months. I'd walk the streets of Naples and see all the sights available to me for free, and then I'd come back by nightfall exhausted, expecting a miracle to happen any day to free me from my cage.

Connecting with the local branch of Youth for Christ was a critical factor in my ability to not only wait it out but to grow spiritually. Experiencing the support of Christ's community to deliver me from feeling trapped and isolated was absolutely necessary. I did not speak Italian, and the only person who spoke English in their office was their secretary, Eleanor Fairchild. She had come on her own initiative with only twenty-five dollars a month support promised by her home church, the Church of the Open Door in Los Angeles. She was there on faith and was toughing it out in her own way. I'd go there several times a week, and we would spend our time in biblical reflection, conversation, and prayer. One day she invited me to have lunch with her. I was most happy to accept, thinking I'd have a decent meal for a change. To my great surprise, she poured out dry cornflakes in two bowls, mixed it with water, and that was it. "Sorry," she said, "but I can't afford milk." The missionaries in Cyprus were always well fed and lived in beautiful homes. This was a different kind of missionary indeed. Again, God was teaching me that my calling was not guaranteed to be lived in prosperity. I have never forgotten Eleanor's witness to me, and her influence in my spiritual growth has been priceless.

Two years later, after I had made it to America, I heard on the religious radio news that she had died in Naples. When I was able to go to Los Angeles, I went to the Church of the Open Door and looked up her mother. I found her in the congregation following the service and proceeded to tell her how much her daughter had influenced my life, and how thankful I was for her sensitive support in my times of need. Then I asked, "What happened to Eleanor? Why did she die? She was only thirty years old."

Her mother's answer shocked and startled me. "I believe she died from malnutrition," she said without filling me in on details.

I was not surprised at her answer, knowing the hardship Eleanor had endured. The hardships did not only relate to physical sustenance but spiritual support as well. I had noticed that she was rather alone in that office and the Italian head of YFC there did not especially appreciate her. Nevertheless she toughed it out because it was her conviction that she was sent there to serve regardless of accompanying circumstances. She continues to be, for me, one who has played a key role in shaping my faith.

For two months my ordeal in Naples continued. My last letter to the university was written in desperation, saying in effect that I was languishing and there was to be no turning back to Cyprus, no matter what the conclusion of this matter would be. A week later I got a copy of a letter Dr. Bob Jones Jr., president of the university, had written to the consul general saying that this matter had grown to the point where they were getting the State Department of the United States involved, and that the Vice-Consul Lewis McCorquodale would be investigated for religious discrimination! It was their contention that when the vice-consul realized that I was coming to a Protestant university to study for the Christian ministry, he sought to block it because he was Roman Catholic in a Roman Catholic nation.

With the copy of this letter in my pocket, I proceeded to the Embassy one more time thinking, "They will probably throw me out for sure and for good this time!" By now, I was a well-known figure there; but to my great surprise, I was not ignored and left to wait and wait, as they did before. This time the secretary ran to the door as soon as she saw me, and assured me that matters had been settled, and that my application for a visa was finally approved (not telling why, of course). She then said, "Within one week you will have your visa and can proceed to travel to America." When I appeared before Mr. McCorquedale, he never looked up at me but signed the papers and bid me farewell. The miracle I was waiting for finally took place. I had my own version of "Free at last! Free at last! Thank God almighty, I'm free at last!"

On October 3, 1949, I embarked on SS. Saturnia with passage to New York City. I had a bunk bed in the lowest possible section, along with over a score of Italians in one room, all immigrating to the United States. Every meal served was spaghetti dished out of big cauldrons and slopped onto plates held out like prisoners waiting in line. It didn't take me long to get sick and to run to the deck for fresh air. There I stayed all day munching on a piece of bread and an orange. It took me a long time after that journey to eat spaghetti again!

Not much of great interest took place on board, except that the Americans among the passengers were listening to the radio with cheers going up from time to time. I was told the baseball World Series was being played between the New York Yankees and the Brooklyn Dodgers. I did not know that much about the game and had little interest in it. However on October 5, the increasing crescendo of cheers and shouts pulled me in, and I watched with great fascination the pandemonium breaking out on the ship's deck. The Yankees pulled it off and won in the fifth and final game. That was not the most excitement that was generated on board during our crossing of the Atlantic Ocean. As the skyline of America began to appear on the horizon, we crowded the railings peering intensely ahead. The passengers began to point into the distance excitedly. "There it is! There it is!" And little by little, the Statue of Liberty came into full view, and before long we passed right by it on our way to the pier. I must confess that I had a lump in my throat and a tear or two trickled down my cheeks in joyful and thankful celebration: "Here at last, here at last. Thank God almighty here at last."

The ship docked at New York City's Forty-Second Street Pier on October 10, 1949. Everyone was hanging over the railings and cheering as we approached the dock, while hundreds of relatives and friends of the passengers were below waving and shouting their welcome. I strained to see if anyone had come for me. Alas, no one.

I arrived in America, exhilarated that I had finally made it, but sad that no one was there for me. In my pocket I had instructions to board a train for Charlottesville, Virginia, where Bob Finley and his family would welcome me. I had just enough money for one night's lodging and a train ticket, with five dollars left over. Upon disembarking the ship, I was told by a taxi driver that a good place to stay that night would be Sloane House YMCA, nearby on Forty-Second Street. When I arrived there, I was told to my dismay at the desk that there was no private room available. Assuming that YMCA was a Christian institution, I thought to ask another man standing in line if he would want to share a room with me. I did so, and he agreed. Consequently, my first night in America was spent in a room with a total stranger. However after we had checked in and settled in our beds, I began to have second thoughts about rooming with a stranger. I discovered that trying to sleep with one eye open was just not possible. All night I worried that this stranger could take off with my belongings and leave me totally helpless!

Having survived my first night in America without incident, I got on a Pennsylvania RR train out of Penn Station, with a ticket to Charlottesville, Virginia. Among the many interesting sights and sounds I encountered, one that stands out is buying a newspaper on board the train. I saw the conductor with papers under his arm; and thinking he was selling them, I offered to buy one.

"Here," he said, handing me the whole bunch. "You can have it for free."

"But I only want one."

"It is only one," he answered.

Welcome to America and the *New York Times*. In Cyprus, the local newspaper was only a folded-over one sheet of paper. But here, it was a bundle. That one paper had been left on a seat, and the conductor had picked it up to discard it. That is but one example of simple and yet profound impressions I began to accumulate from day one in America.

I traveled through a literal wonderland of lush green scenery of rivers and woods, towns and cities, until I arrived in Charlottesville several hours later. What a relief and joy it was to see Bob Finley on the platform waiting to greet me. A journey that had begun on August 5 finally came to a happy ending on October 12, 1949. I recalled the words of the great hymn, "Amazing Grace": "Through many dangers, toils, and snares, I have already come; 'tis grace has brought me safe thus far, and grace will lead me home." I had arrived at a substation called Charlottesville (actually I was headed to the village of Free Union, sixteen miles to the northwest), my new home in America, on my grand journey "home" which has not yet ended.

A Maturing Family

My parents Manuel and Martha, 1956.

The four Kassounis, in the barley field behind our house, ca. 1935. *Fourth and youngest, me.*

Family photo, ca. 1940.

Our family on our front porch, ca. 1946. *Back, fourth from left,* me.

My Education

1. American Academy student body, ca. 1948. *Inset photo,* my parents and me.
2. Posing with my high school field hockey team *(center, back row)* and our coach Mr. G. Chopourian *(far right).*
3. The American Academy, revisited in 2010.
4. Our high school graduating class of 1949. *Center front,* Dr. W.W. Weir, our principal; *seated to his left in white suit,* Mr. G. Chopourian, class sponsor; *directly behind,* me. *Top row, fourth from the left,* Karnig Berberian; *second from the right,* Levon Melkonian.

My Friends and Faith Community

1. My Scout Troop at the American Academy, 1948. *Center, no hat, me.*
2. Our church leaders with youth and families, ca. 1945. *Top row: seventh from the left, me; second from the right,* brother Sarkis. *In front of Sarkis, in big hat,* sister Nouvart; *to her right,* sister Agnes. *Standing in front of me,* father Manuel. *Seated in front of Manuel, with the high forehead,* Rev. Y. Mugar.
3. Bob Finley, my spiritual mentor, introducing me to the congregation of Mt. Olivet Presbyterian Church on my first Sunday in America, October 9, 1949.
4. Eleanor Fairchild, missionary with Youth for Christ, with me and a friend in Naples, Italy, when I was "stuck" there for two months.

Three

GROWING AND OUTGROWING

My life in America began by being warmly welcomed into the Finley household. Their home in Free Union, VA was a farmhouse in a rural community within a cluster of other farms in view of each other and located at the base of the beautiful Blue Ridge Mountains, a few miles to the west. The patriarch was Walter, always called "Dad," and the matriarch was Melissa, always called "Mom." The farm had seen better days and did no longer produce much by way of crops. The sons and daughters pitched in to support their parents and got together often for reunions and celebrations. I was immediately welcomed into their circle as a member of the family, and from then on this became my home away from home.

My multifaceted education began with my first church service, in Olivet Presbyterian Church in Charlottesville, where Bob was speaking. I was asked to share a few thoughts and my testimony. I noticed that the balcony was filled with blacks, but the main floor had only whites. I had never seen anything like that. In answer to my inquiry as to why it was so, I was told: "In the South we have segregation of the races. Negroes do not sit with whites in church or any other public function." I learned the meaning of the word "segregation," and from there on, it was in prominent display all over the South, including Bob Jones University.

College: Amazing Years

My arrival at BJU (Bob Jones University) in Greenville, South Carolina, came a month after school had already started. I did not know that my case of intentionally delayed entry into America had become a "*cause celebre*" and that announcements had been made periodically at chapel about its progress. Upon my arrival at the chapel service (at which time the entire student body of over two thousand students were present), I was introduced to the assembly, and the auditorium went up in a loud cheer! Chalk one up for the triumph of Protestant faith and perseverance over Catholic attempts to thwart my entry into America.

That first chapel service was amazing in one other way. I had never in my life been in a room with that many Protestants present. In Cyprus, having been in a minority all my life (Armenian in Cyprus, and Protestant among the Armenians), we had developed what I call a "minority complex." I had never been in a group with more than a hundred Protestants present before. I was overwhelmed by the sight of it, and most of all, by the sound of two thousand voices singing "O for a Thousand Tongues to Sing My Dear Redeemer's Name." I thought I had died and gone to heaven!

The school had intentionally nurtured its image, calling itself the World's Most Unusual University. It even had a radio station with the call letters WMUU. My four years at BJU were highly significant in the formation of my identity and the direction of my life and ministry. This involved not only positive action in appreciation and agreement but also eventual reaction and rejection of their fundamentalist mentality and agenda. I devote a significant amount of space in this book to this period in my life because of this fact. For me, this has been an outstanding case of contradictory and also complementary points of life coming together in a Christian community.

The school was founded as a college in 1927 in Florida by Bob Jones Sr., an evangelist in the style of Billy Sunday. His avowed vision was to train evangelists to cover America and bring the country back to loyalty to Jesus Christ. The college moved to Cleveland, Tennessee, in 1937 and then to its present location in Greenville, South Carolina, in 1947, where it grew from being a college to being a university. In 1949, when I arrived there, Bob Jones Sr. was very much alive and in control of the University's life and destiny, even though his son Bob Jones Jr. was the president. Dr. Bob Jones Sr. preached at many of our chapel services. With his old-fashioned style of rant, rave, and cajole, he tried to instill his brand of Christianity in us. There were several themes that he repeated, I believe intentionally, so that psychologically the students became disciples under his control. Most of the men, including me, were Bible majors, intending to become evangelists, in accordance with his dream. They were called "preacher boys" and listened to him with rapt attention. He was, what I believe to be, the last of the old-style southern evangelists of the late nineteenth and early twentieth century.

Dr. Bob Jones Jr. was quite different in style but totally in sync with his father. He was polished in speech, not as demonstrative in preaching style, and intentionally cultured. He had succeeded in adding to old-fashioned Southern-style brimstone and hell-fire theology a layer of education and culture. For example, we had an "Artist Series" of concerts and events featuring nationally known vocalists and instrumentalists. He himself was a Shakespearian actor. The school's drama department, under his tutelage, staged a number of Shakespeare's plays. He had a very good museum established on campus, with a number of European and other outstanding art pieces. His pet theme was that fundamentalism in America needed to get rid of its backward-country image and develop polish and sophistication. He succeeded to some extent and was to be commended for it, although at times it was rather humorous. For example, he had the drama department produce a film of Shakespeare's *Macbeth*, with him playing the lead role. Critics joked about his southern accent in a Scottish setting.

The themes that Dr. Bob Sr. repeated constantly in chapel and sought to drill into us were a mixture of moral and conservative theology and ecclesiastical ideology. A sampling of his sayings which I have kept are listed below:

"Do right till the stars fall."

"You can do anything you ought to do."

"The door to the room of success swings on the hinges of opposition."

"When gratitude dies on the altar of a man's heart, that man is well-nigh hopeless."

"It is one thing to know there is a God; it's another thing to know the God that is."

"Jesus never taught men how to make a living. He taught men how to live."

"It is at the Cross I get the power to live the Sermon on the Mount."

Woven into the fabric of Bob Jones University was ecclesiastical ideology that sought to pull students away from their denominational loyalties. The University tolerated no criticism and had its own ecclesiastic hierarchy, whose head was Dr. Bob Jones Sr., and of course his son as well. The faculty was totally committed in loyalty, and any who dared take exception to the position taken by the Joneses on any theological or social issue soon were let go. Many times the ringing call was "Do not let your 'religio-politico bosses' tell you what to preach or to do," in reference to ministers going into various denominations, such as the Presbyterian Church. Often they were painted as being apostate and anti-Christian, with warning that we would come under their destructive control if we allowed it. What became evident to me, however, was that they themselves were in their own way "religio-politico bosses." They had their own ecclesiastical council that received and ordained candidates to the Christian ministry.

This amounted to being a denomination in itself. Dr. Bob Sr. used to say that the Methodist Church offered him a bishopric, if he would agree to join them (he was from Alabama), but he refused, choosing rather to be independent. What followed, however, is that he became a bishop anyway, but this time over his own self-created religious community composed of faculty, students, and alumni.

Financial support for my tuition and board came from an anonymous donor, with a monthly donation of one hundred dollars to BJU in my behalf, and twenty-five dollars a month in work/scholarship aid from the school. Total tuition and board was less than $2,000 a year. However, Bob Finley had secured a benefactor for me whose instruction was that I was not to know his identity until I graduated. My hunch was that this would prevent me from going to him for more support as needs arose. Four years later, after his identity was given to me, I personally visited him and thanked him profusely for his great generosity. He was Mr. Earl Vaughn, who owned the coal company in Charlottesville, Virginia.

My work/scholarship paid me, and others, only thirty cents an hour. Every morning I joined a cleanup work crew at 5:30 a.m. to clean the offices of both Bob Jones Sr. and Jr. and of others in the administration building. What stands out in my memory is the big, elaborately hand-carved olive-wood desk that Bob Jones Jr. had brought from the Holy Land which was his pride and joy. There was hardly any money available to me for incidentals, and even some necessities. Three prepaid meals a day at the school dining room was all I had, with each meal lasting only twenty minutes. Needless to say, I gobbled up as much food as I could, for I was always hungry!

Academic life came easy for me, and I had no problem with any of the courses majoring in the Bible, as a preseminarian. Even though others planned to go directly into evangelistic ministry, my sights were set on graduate school and further education, in planning to enter the ordained ministry. I had no idea where I would go for this or what denomination I would join. On campus, I was a member of a group of Presbyterians who met Sunday mornings for Bible study and prayers, since back home I was a member of the Reformed Presbyterian Church.

Dorm life in Graves Hall was cramped and interesting. My roommate, along with five others, was Allen Finley, Bob's "kid brother," as he was called. He and I formed a close friendship that lasted a lifetime. I was his best man in his wedding to Ruth Goodwin in 1953 in Los Angeles. We played on the same soccer team in college, and we often went on preaching missions together. Sometimes, in jest, he would imitate Billy Graham, and I his soloist, George Beverly Shea.

Ministerial Boot Camp

Our training to be evangelists included forming teams and going out every weekend to preach wherever we could, be it street, jail, hospital, or church (if they would have us, since Bob Jones's "preacher boys" were suspect as being too extreme to fit regular church services!). Our assignment was to come back and write a report for our evangelism-related class.

My first experience preaching a short sermon took place in a chain gang in Georgia. I was an ignorant immigrant not aware of the South's penal institutions. It was Sunday afternoon, and the prisoners were all on their beds resting. But to my amazement, they were all chained, with a long chain running through each prisoner's leg iron all the way across to the wall and locked on the opposite side. At the conclusion of my short message, I gave the call for a response of commitment to Jesus Christ, and one black man raised his hand. The guard unlocked the chain, pulled it through till he could be released, and then he was allowed to come out and meet with me concerning his decision for Christ. So, this man was my first convert in America. After a week or two, we lost touch, and I have no idea what happened to him thereafter.

Every possible weekend was spent in some kind of preaching, witnessing, and communicating the Gospel. Upon our return to the campus, we submitted a report to our professor on evangelism. It was expected that we should report on how many people had made "decisions to accept Christ." Reporting no such results would affect our grade negatively. Our efforts took us to places such as prisons, juvenile detention centers, rescue missions, parks, and even street corners. As a result of the variety of experiences, I developed my ability to speak in public and to present my messages forcefully and clearly. This is the one special skill I gained at BJU that I have treasured immensely, and for which I am most thankful. It has served me well in the dozen or so churches I have served. The maxim drilled into us was "Speak up to be heard clearly by all. Otherwise, you may just as well never stand up to speak."

Bob Jones University was part and parcel with the culture of the South, central to which was segregation of races. I learned about this little by little. With growing amazement, I observed a great divide between what they claimed by way of the Bible and Christ-centered theology, and their practice denying the very essence of the Gospel. The school was totally segregated and did not include any blacks (or Negroes as they were called then). Blacks had to sit in the back of the bus. Public places had separate facilities for whites and blacks. Bob Jones's leaders never addressed this practice, and life went along without any protest or discussion about it. Finally, it became evident to me that BJU was an institution totally committed to segregation, and my personal hunch was that probably money flowed into its coffers from Southern institutions because of their stand on race.

One incident that left an indelible mark on my conscience was while our evangelistic team was on a mission in Greenville. We went to a bar run by black owners, with all black customers. The irony of it was that the culture would not prevent whites from going to a black bar, but the reverse was not possible. Actually, Bob Jones Sr. would say, "If you want easy decisions for Christ to result from your preaching, go out there and talk to a Negro." We asked the owner if we could have five minutes for a quick service, and then we would leave. He agreed to it, made the announcement that "the preacher boys are here so quiet down and listen." One of us played a trumpet solo, one gave a minute testimony, and one preached a two-minute sermon. At the end the invitation for commitment to Christ was made and those interested were invited to come out and talk to us. One young man did so and came outside.

"Yes," he said, "I want to accept Christ as my Savior."

"Wonderful!" we said. "Let's talk about it."

"Not only do I want to be a Christian, but I want to study to be a preacher, just like you," he replied.

Again our response was one of great appreciation. However, we soon realized that he had laid a trap for us.

"I want to go to Bob Jones University just like you," he said.

"We're sorry, but BJU does not accept Negroes," we sadly replied.

"You can take your Jesus, then, and get out of here!" He retorted sharply.

It was eighteen years later, in 1971, that BJU first admitted blacks into its student body; and thirty-seven years after that (in 2008), it apologized publicly for its racist policies. Well and good, but what about all the harm done to the cause of Christ and the many people hurt and abused in the process of BJU claiming authority for their biased policies from the Bible? Here is a vivid example of how American Christian fundamentalism has blind spots and is logically unable or ethically unwilling to acknowledge their serious flaws.

My life on campus was rather drab, since I had no money to entertain friends and no girlfriends, except those we talked with during meals and after classes. We had cultural events on campus to which we could invite girls and then walk them home slowly to their dorms along what was called "The Snail Trail." No holding of hands, no kissing, or any other physical touch was allowed. Bob Jones Sr. used to brag publicly that BJU had never sent a girl home disgraced because of sexual misconduct (meaning pregnancy). I know of one student, by the name of Hal Taylor (an Armenian from Fresno), who was "shipped home" (an expression used on campus meaning expulsion) because he was caught kissing a girl in a broom closet!

Sports were my source for much-needed emotional and physical exercise, centered in soccer and tennis. We had sixteen "societies," like fraternities, who competed against each other in intramural sports. I played center forward on Pi Gamma Delta's team, and Allen Finley played full back. We won most of our games, since the majority of the players had never played soccer before. Our center line was formed by the dynamic four: three of us from Cyprus, including Levon Melkonian and Levon Yergatian, and one from Greece, Elias Moscovis. I kicked all of the penalty shots and never missed in four years, except for one. During the final play of the final game with no time left, I kicked a miserable shot that hardly even reached the goalkeeper. So ended my glorious career in soccer! I have often used that incident as a lesson I learned (or I think I did) in humility. Proverbs says, "Let him who thinks that he stands take heed lest he fall." And fall I did!

Summers on the Road

Since financial restrictions prevented me from returning home for the summer breaks, I had to find creative alternatives. In the summer of 1950, Fuad BahBah and I teamed up to speak in churches about the Middle East. He was from Ramallah, Palestine, and a Pentecostal. He proceeded to set up our speaking engagements, by requesting fellow students to write to their pastors about us. Most were in Pentecostal churches, but there were a number of other denominations also included. Thus, I had an excellent first-hand experience in learning and encountering church life in America.

We traveled by hitchhiking to our destinations in sixteen states in the south, midwest, and north. Since we traveled "by faith," we found ourselves on lonely highways from time to time, wondering if we would make it in time to our appointed services. I learned to sing, often and with prayers, "I trust in God, wherever I may be, upon the land, or on the rolling sea. For come what may, from day to day, my heavenly Father watches over me." It is rather amazing that we never missed an appointment!

We received free-will offerings following our talks, which finally enabled us to ride the bus back to South Carolina from Virginia in time for the new school year. We spoke mostly at Sunday evening and Wednesday night services, giving our life stories and testimonies. Pentecostal services were puzzling and confusing for me. With great astonishment I watched people interrupt the sermon with their direct "messages from

God," which they called "prophecies," speaking in unknown tongues followed by "interpretations." People danced, and some fell or fainted in the aisles, the sick got "healed," and order was seemingly lost. Very un-Presbyterian indeed. What amazes me is that today the fastest growing church denomination is the Assemblies of God, the very same church Fuad BahBah belonged to. Along the way, there were a number of them who tried to convert me into joining their ranks. Discussions on the meaning of being "Anointed with the Holy Spirit" took place in conjunction with our speaking engagements. Alas, to no avail.

My second summer (1951) was spent in Springfield, Ohio. Larry Shackelford, a fellow student at BJU, invited me to stay with his family there and find summer jobs for us both. Also, his pastor agreed to have us help out as temporary youth leaders in their Blessed Baptist Church.

We found employment at the Crowell-Collier Publishing Co. as "book-catchers." The magazines, *Women's Home Companion, Collier,* and others were published there. Huge presses churned out sections non-stop, and it was our job to catch and stack them in neat rows. If we did not act fast enough, they would pile up and soon drop to the floor, and then we'd be in big trouble. We would pray that the presses would stop, because of some malfunction or other, allowing us extra time for rest.

Getting a paycheck at the end of the week was most exciting indeed. I was so proud of myself that I went to Western Union and cabled my first paycheck (I think it was seventy-five dollars) to my father back home. Years later, when I applied for US citizenship, I got into big trouble because I had worked for pay that year with no work permit issued to me first.

Blessed Hope Baptist Church was a member of a fundamentalist denomination called the General Association of Regular Baptists. (We called it the "Grand Army of Rebellious Baptists.") Every Sunday morning they sang "Happy Birthday" to those celebrating their day. However, that song was then followed by their own version: "Happy Birthday to you. Only one will not do. Born again means salvation. How many have you?" Nevertheless, the people were most friendly and accepted me without hesitation, assuming that anyone from BJU must be okay. We had some great times leading the youth program throughout that summer.

During my last Sunday, I was invited to share a few thoughts at the pulpit. After thanking them for their love and support I said, "I have held a secret from you all summer, but I am now ready to share it with you." They all perked up with interest. "I am not a Baptist but a Presbyterian," I confessed. "Let me give you two reasons why I waited till this moment to let you know. The first is that you probably would have objected to having me lead your youth, if you knew I was not Baptist. The second reason is that for the rest of your lives I want you to remember that you have met at least one Presbyterian who was alive in Christ and as excited about the Gospel as you are. There are many more like me out there. We are all one in Christ!" How's that for a grass-roots demonstration of ecumenicity? In those days I did not even know what that word meant.

Alas, I have lost touch with Larry and can't locate him anywhere. I called the church office when I was in Ohio two years ago, and the minister said, "We have no record here of a Shackelford family, sorry."

For my third summer (1952), Allen Finley and I talked seriously about forming a team and going to the Middle East on an evangelistic mission together. I corresponded with Rev. Hagop Sagherian, my former pastor in Larnaca who was now in Beirut, Lebanon. He was delighted with the idea and encouraged us to proceed with our plans. He was a leader in the Union of Armenian Evangelical Churches and the pastor of the church in Ashrafieh. He arranged for us to be the speakers at a number of churches and two conference centers.

Knowing the importance of music for a team like ours, we invited Dick Knox, a very good trombone player and song leader, to join us. This he did. He convinced me to buy a trombone (I paid twenty-five dollars for a much-used instrument) and volunteered to teach me how to play just enough to perform duets together. I agreed reluctantly and dragged that instrument everywhere but never learned to play it right. It always sounded like a fog-horn! I finally gave it away to charity years later.

We booked passage to Europe on the maiden voyage of the new liner SS United States. It was a beautiful and very fast ship, whose top speed was kept a state secret. We made it across the Atlantic to Le Havre, France, in record speed, arriving a day early. In the meantime, Allen came down with mumps, and we were worried he would be quarantined, so we wrapped him up with a scarf and led him ashore. We headed to the European Bible Institute in Paris, where friends took charge of his recovery. From there, Dick and I went on to Greece, and on to Beirut, where Allen joined us later.

During this trip to the Middle East we took a few days off and traveled by a large taxi to the Holy Land, via Damascus, Amman, and eventually Jerusalem. A number of incidents happened along the way that are worth telling here. The three of us were seated in the second row, and the other passengers were in the back seat. On the way to Damascus, the radio kept playing on and on in a monotone, which we assumed were Arabic songs. We made comments to each other about how boring that was and how seemingly endless they were. Then, a man in the back seat spoke up in very clear English, saying "What you are hearing are recitations from the Koran, and we would appreciate it if you did not make jokes about it!" He was the son of some big shot in Amman and returning after studying abroad. We apologized profusely and from then on were very silent indeed. At the border crossing to Syria, I was separated from my two friends and asked to come in to speak with the officers. I sat in a chair with several interrogators standing next to me. They asked me questions about who I was, what nationality I had, and why was I traveling with Americans. Since my passport was from Cyprus, was I not really some kind of informer or spy? They would then speak to me in Arabic and watch to see if I understood what they were saying, since I had told them I was Armenian and did not speak Arabic.

Finally, they said, "You must know that we are smart, and you cannot fool us."

While I was filled with fear inside, I calmly responded, "Of course I know you are very intelligent men. It is precisely for that reason you must understand that I am telling you the truth!"

They were either convinced by my great logic, or they were merely putting a scare in me, but they let me go on my way after that.

When we were asked by a soldier at the checkpoint to open our luggage, we realized that in loading our suitcases we had made a big mistake. We had filled in all the available spaces with Gospel tracts, and we were in a Muslim country. However many of them were in Armenian. Upon seeing this, the soldier said in Armenian to me, "Are you Armenian?" He was Armenian also! "Quick, close it up and go," he ordered, thus saving us from another painful episode with the interrogators.

Our next "crisis" took place in Jerusalem, two days later. We stayed in the dormitory of the school belonging to St. George Angelical Cathedral, in the old city. Looking out of our window, we could see Jordanian soldiers patrolling the road leading to the Israeli sector close by, since the wars in 1947 had created the State of Israel and separated the country and the Holy City. St. George Cathedral was on the Jordanian side, and traffic across the border was nonexistent. Tensions ran very high, and both authorities were on high alert.

We walked right into the jaws of this problem one morning. Krikor Tashjian, one of three brothers who were members of the Armenian Brotherhood church there, volunteered to guide us on a tour of the city. As we were walking in the city along the city wall, we were not aware that the other side was Israeli controlled. In an opening in the wall filled with barbed wire was a sign in broken English cautioning all to stay away. I pointed to the sign with a comment, and immediately there was a shout from the top of the wall. An angry Jordanian soldier was aiming his gun at us and threatening to shoot! We spoke no Arabic, hence had no idea what he was saying. However, our guide did, and he at once responded and kept talking to pacify the soldier. He finally convinced him that we were mere tourists, innocent of any sinister intention, and pleaded to let us go. To our great relief, he finally did, and we got out of there fast. That was a trip to remember!

Back in Lebanon, we were scheduled to speak at Christian Endeavor youth conferences. One was outside Beirut, called KCHAG (meaning

Christian Endeavor Center). This center was the pride of the Evangelical community. It had several buildings and a nice chapel, for year-round camping, conferences, and lectures. The other center was in the northwestern corner of Syria, near the border of Turkey. There were two small Armenian villages called Koerkuneh-Ekyzoluk (near the historic town of Kessab). This is the region made famous by the resistance against the Ottoman Turks during the Genocide of 1915. They all retreated to the mountain called Mousa Dagh (the Mountain of Moses) and held it for weeks until they were rescued by a French cruiser whose lookouts spotted the SOS sign put up in desperation. This struggle is immortalized in the novel by Franz Werfel titled, *Forty Days of Mousa Dagh*. Youth from the local churches as well as from the interior, mostly Aleppo, came for a week-long conference where we were the featured speakers. The village had no electricity or running water. We slept on dirt floors, and we went at midnight a hundred yards away to one pipe with running water for very cold sponge baths only. We did it at night to make sure no women from the village would be coming to get water for their houses.

Dick Knox had a real problem with this arrangement, because he had never shaved without an electric razor. In every country we went we had to find a transformer so his electric razor would work. In Cyprus, we even had one built for him because none could be found in the stores.

He was a trooper, however. He began to shave with a regular razor, but alas, his soft white skin could not take it, and his face turned into what looked like raw hamburger.

On the spiritual side of things, however, we were very effective in proclaiming the good news of the Gospel. As a result, quite a number of youth made decisions for Christ.[2]

After two days there, I had to cut my trip short to return to America, because school was ready to start and the authorities had refused me permission to miss several days of classes. Al and Dick, having already graduated, stayed on for continuing ministries there. Eventually, they

---

2   See Appendix 2 for a letter of commendation from Dr. Bob Jones Jr.

went to Cyprus for extended evangelistic rallies there. Dick did return to America but became a self-appointed missionary in Cyprus and Lebanon.

He became increasingly controversial in style and theology, creating dissention among the very same good folks who had welcomed him and supported him. Among these were my sister Nouvart and her husband, Hercules. They were key leaders of the evangelical community in Cyprus.

Years later, in 1969, when I was invited to work among our churches in Beirut for five weeks, with one week in each of the five churches, I called Dick (who was living there at the time) and requested his help in bringing some special music to our gatherings. This he refused to do, saying that he could not cooperate in any church affiliated with the World Council of Churches. And all these churches were. They were the very same churches that had first welcomed him, back in 1953, and because of their support he gained a foothold there for his future separatist work. I was so shocked by his stance that I said, "I'm sorry I ever introduced you to these good folks. You'll never hear from me again!" And so we parted ways.

Allen Finley, following his ministry in Cyprus, was invited to head the San Francisco branch of International Students Inc. (ISI), the continuing ministry to overseas students started by his brother Bob Finley (my mentor/benefactor). He was later invited to head a missions organization called Christian Nationals Evangelism Commission (CNEC), centered mainly in the Far East. When its scope increased to include many countries around the world, its name changed to Partners International. Under his skilled and sensitive direction, this mission organization grew to include scores of countries and thousands of churches and educational institutions operated by indigenous peoples.

Life After College
While Al and Dick stayed on in the Middle East, I had to return to college for my final year at BJU. I concentrated on making sure I completed my classes and prepared to go to a graduate school for theological

training. I was in touch with a group of Armenian Evangelical leaders on the East Coast. Among them was my cousin, Dr. Dicran Kassouny, who was the pastor of the Armenian Martyrs' Congregational Church of Philadelphia, Pennsylvania, and Rev. G. Diran Minassian, who was the Director of Youth Ministries of the Armenian Evangelical Union. They negotiated with me to come to New York City to attend New York Biblical Seminary and also to be the youth leader of the Armenian Presbyterian Church, West New York, New Jersey. I agreed, and so my course was set for the next three years.

Through my cousin, Dr. Dicran, and Mrs. Arousiag "Roushie" Kassouny, I established contact with Armenians again, from whom I had been isolated for three years. He was the son of my uncle, the Rev. Yeghia Kassouny, and pastor of the Armenian Martyrs' Congregational Church in Philadelphia. I spent many of my holidays at their home, attended their church, and began to form friendships with their youth group. They had a very fine and talented number of college-age young people who knew how to have a vibrant and dynamic organization.

Marriage and More

Among the youth of the church was Adrine Keshishian, the second daughter of Misak and Siroun Keshishian. She and her sister Esther were very active and popular youth leaders. Adrine was a student of nursing at the University of Pennsylvania. I was made to feel very welcome in their home, especially after I learned that their mother, Siroun, had lived in Cyprus and at one time was my sister Nouvart's elementary school teacher.

My attraction and love for Adrine (Addie) grew and grew, until I asked her to marry me, which she eventually did! Our wedding took place in their church on August 28, 1954. It was a bold move on our part because we had no money. I had a summer job working as a janitor in the facilities of Faith Seminary in a suburb of the city. My sister, Agnes, was a student there and had spoken a good word for me, so I got the job. I was twenty-three and thinking I was an old man already because all my friends, such as Allen Finley, were already married. Based mostly on faith and love, we embarked on our future together. Our honeymoon was in a Pocono Mountain resort. Having no car to get us there, we bought seats in a bus full of young people going to their summer camp. Needless to say we took the bench seats at the very back of the bus.

We established residency in the Biblical Seminary quarters in New York City, until we had to move when Addie became pregnant. I searched all over lower Manhattan for an apartment, to no avail. We were getting quite discouraged, and plans were afoot to have her move back to Philadelphia with her parents temporarily. But then a "miracle" took place. I got a call from Mrs. Dewey at the receptionist desk, informing us that she had received a call from a Mrs. Petersen in Forest Hills offering to share her house with a seminary couple in need of housing. We jumped for joy! We moved into her beautiful house in toney Forest Hills and continued living there until my graduation in 1956.

Seminary and Family

The Biblical Seminary of New York (now renamed New York Theological Seminary) was established in 1911 by Dr. Wilbur White. His vision was to maintain inductive study and teaching in the Bible itself and make that the focus of the curriculum, rather than theological and philosophical studies. In those days biblical studies were being de-emphasized in theological institutions around the country. At Biblical Seminary I gained the skills necessary to first go to the Scriptures directly, rather than to commentaries, to gain knowledge and insights needed for preaching and teaching. Such skills have served me well over the years.

The seminary was located at 235 East Forty-Ninth Street in a twelve-story building housing everything from a basketball gymnasium (basement), to auditorium, classrooms, sleeping quarters, dining hall, and volleyball court (on the roof). Thus, we did not need to leave the building at all, except for shopping and field assignments. I graduated from Biblical Seminary in 1956, earning the Master of Divinity degree (MDiv).

Our home was blessed with four children, three girls and a boy. Our first child, Linda Joy was born on June 7, 1955, in the University of Pennsylvania Hospital, the same institution where Addie had received her training as a nurse. Our second daughter, Nancy Jean, was also born in the same hospital on June 22, 1958. Our third daughter, Karen Martha, was born on November 14, 1960, in the North Shore Hospital, Long Island; and so was our son, Timothy Vartkes, born on May 29, 1963. Addie worked as a visiting nurse in lower Manhattan during our first year, and I worked in the Seminary Library on a part-time basis during the week and as Youth Leader in the Armenian Presbyterian Church of West New York, New Jersey, on Sundays. Thus, we earned enough to keep us going, and raising a young family.

University Years

Vartkes
Kassouni

1. Bob Jones University, 1953. Bible majors of the student body.
2. Dr. Bob Jones Jr., visiting with my parents in Larnaca, 1951.
3. Our Mission to the Middle East Team, 1952, including *(left to right):* me, Dick Knox, Allen Finley, and Dr. W.W. Weir.
4. Our Mission Team and friends stranded with a flat tire, on the way to Kessab, Syria.

Seminary Years

Faculty and leaders, Armenian C. E. Inter State Union Retreat, May 1, 1954. *Front row, second and third from left,* Rev. Puzant Kalfayan and Rev. Diran Minassian. *In back row:* Marie Albarian, Rev. George Paboojian, Ann Darpinian, Louise Meacham, me, and Dr. John Markarian.

Biblical Seminary of New York, student body, 1955. *Front row, first on the left,* me.

A New Family

Adrine Keshishian,
my former wife.

Adrine with her sister Esther,
mother Siroon, and father Misak.

Adrine and me.

With our first child, Linda Joy.

Our Children

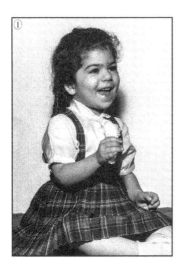

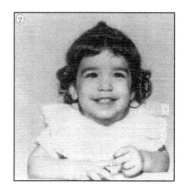

1. Child 1, Linda Joy.
2. Child 2, Nancy Jean.
3. Linda and Nancy together.
4. Child 3, Karen Martha.
5. Child 4, Timothy Vartkes.

Four

Into the World

Out of My Cocoon

After graduating from Seminary in 1956, our family moved back to Philadelphia, where I was invited by Bob Finley to join the organization he had founded, International Students Inc., headquartered in Washington, DC. My assignment was to open a branch office in Philadelphia and run it as its area director.

Prior to that, we had been hoping to go to Syria as mission workers. I was invited to go to Aleppo, Syria to develop and direct the youth programs of the Armenian Evangelical churches. The Armenian Missionary Association of America had made all the arrangements, and their director, the Rev. Puzant Kalfayan, had already booked passage for us in a merchant ship bound for Beirut. However, in 1956 Great Britain led the invasion of Egypt, their objective being the capture of the Suez Canal. Since I was still a citizen of Cyprus, carrying a British passport, the door to our entry into Syria was shut tight, and so we were open to new ministries; hence, my call to join ISI, which I did.

My two years in that ministry got me involved with international students studying in the Philadelphia area. Our plan was to introduce the students to American families and arrange social and intellectual gatherings, where we would exchange ideas and carry on discussions about our various religions, countries, and cultures.

We opened our office near the University of Pennsylvania, and it became the center of personal and group interaction with a variety of students. Our focus was to share the gospel of Jesus Christ while respecting their religious beliefs and extending to them genuine hospitality and support. I was challenged beyond my expectations, and sometimes beyond my intellectual abilities. Men and women from China, Korea, Japan, India, the Middle East, and Europe mingled with each other, exchanging ideas, beliefs, and convictions. They were sharp and highly motivated people who were nevertheless lonely in a foreign country and seeking friendships and connections with Americans. They would gladly join in gatherings in the homes of local church folks that I had recruited as hosts. We would gather for dinners, picnics, and birthday parties, with discussions always included.

Religious practices always had to be considered in food preparation. Most Hindus did not eat meat. Some ate chicken and fish but not beef. Some did not even eat eggs.

"How can I eat the embryo of a chicken?" one strict vegetarian once asked me.

I replied, "When you put it that way, maybe I will not eat eggs anymore either."

Muslims would eat no pork, Hindus would eat no meat, and Jains would eat nothing (unless they were in charge of everything concerning food). In contrast, Chinese, Koreans, and Japanese had hardly any qualms about food, which was a welcome change for us. My wife would have quite a time preparing meals, as one can expect. But somehow we did it and became quite good at it. Once we put on an authentic Indian meal, with Indian students preparing it. We sat on the floor and ate with our hands. It was quite an experience. However, I kept digging curry out of my fingernails and cuticles for days afterward.

The students were a study in contrast. We had highly intellectual Germans who talked in philosophical terms I could hardly understand.

We had Brahmin (high caste) and low caste "untouchable" Hindus mingling together, sharing their ideas which sometimes revealed their cultural divides. During a gathering of local people and overseas students, a Christian Indian from Kerala State said, "I was an untouchable, but Jesus touched me, and I experienced the love of God. That's why I am now a Christian."

Once I led a group of them on an overnight trip to Lancaster County to meet some Mennonites and Amish folk. We stayed in a house with enough beds for everyone. All, except an African student and me. There was only one double bed left for us two. Needless to say I had a problem crawling in bed with another man and an African at that! However, he had no problem. He wrapped himself in a blanket, like a hot dog in a bun, and promptly went to sleep. I stayed awake for quite some time thinking of how my prejudices had asserted themselves, and praying to God for forgiveness. That was a lesson well learned.

In Philadelphia there were two students living together with whom I developed a close friendship. One was Orhan "Sonny" Dervish, a Turk from Cyprus, who had also attended the American Academy and remembered me faintly from my high school days. He was a Muslim but a secular one. We had talks about Islam and Christianity without each trying to overwhelm the other with religious zeal. We kept up our friendship for several years. When we moved to New York, he was there also and would often visit our home. At times he even baby sat for our children, so Addie and I would go out on occasion. How about that! An Armenian family entrusting their children to a Turk! When we moved to California, we lost contact, and all attempts to locate him have failed.

The other student was Bhisham Bhakshi, a Brahmin Hindu from Bombay and a brilliant aspiring engineer. He had a keen mind and genuine interest in Christianity. He and Sonny would come by my office and just "hang out" as the saying goes. The friendship we developed has lasted all these many years. Actually, he looked me up about thirty years ago and reestablished our contact in California after years of silence between us. He went on from Philadelphia back to India and worked for the Indian Oil Company, eventually becoming its president. He and his lovely wife, Binoo, became close friends of ours. They visited California several times and have been our house guests. Unfortunately, he succumbed to cancer and died in 2015. In his passing I lost a dear friend indeed. They have two sons, Simran and Bambi ("Luv"), whose exploits and challenges were a real concern for their parents, and in whose behalf I volunteered to be of as much help as possible. They called me "Uncle Kass" and often turned to me for support. I will have more to say about this in a later chapter.

Into the Mainstream

On January 20, 1957, I was ordained to the Christian Ministry by the Congregational Christian Association of New York City in the sanctuary of the Armenian Evangelical Church of New York. I was sponsored by the renowned Rev. A. A. Bedikian, pastor emeritus of that church. My cousin, the Rev. Dr. Dicran Y. Kassouny, was the pastor there at the time. The meeting of the Association, where I was examined for ordination, took place in the magnificent Broadway Congregational Church at the northern tip of Times Square. It was a theologically very liberal Association, and I knew I was going to have a tough time there. Along with me were two other candidates to be examined also. They were graduates of Union Seminary, and I was a graduate of New York Biblical Seminary. They preceded me in their examination. In their opening statements, each declared that he was unitarian in his theology. When my turn came, my opening statement was, "I am trinitarian in my theology," and then I proceeded to present my beliefs emanating from that central tenet of faith. Well! The other candidates passed through with no arguments whatsoever, but I was grilled pretty hard for hanging on to a traditional affirmation of faith in the Triune God. At one point an old clergy member of the group stood up and said in a clear voice, "I have been attending this Association for years. I thank God that finally I have heard a young candidate take his stand and affirm his faith in the historical doctrine of the deity of Christ!"

After my ordination, our family moved to Upper Darby, Pennsylvania, and we continued our work with International Students Inc.: I, as the director of the Philadelphia office, while Addie helped out with the office and care of students. We worshiped at the Beverly Hills Presbyterian Church, where Dr. Roy Grace was the pastor. He began to call on me to assist him and then to teach the Collegians Bible Class on Sunday mornings. He kept after me to join the United Presbyterian Church, the denomination to which the local church belonged, saying, "Come join us because you are Presbyterian in heritage anyway." I finally agreed, and with his full support I was received as a ministerial member. Some months later the United Presbyterian Church merged with the Presbyterian Church, United States of America, forming the United Presbyterian Church, United States of America. On January 13, 1959, in a formal ceremony in Philadelphia in which I participated, two streams of clergy walked in separate lines toward each other, merged into one stream, and walked into the sanctuary of Bethany Temple Presbyterian Church for a grand celebration of the new church now united. In 1982 the Southern Presbyterian Church (Presbyterian Church United States) merged with this body and formed the Presbyterian Church (United States of America). Thus the great division which had ripped the church apart during the Civil War was finally ended. I have been a member of this church ever since and have served a number of parishes in this capacity.

Early Colleagues

1. Allen Finley and I: College buddies and friends from then on.
2. Ruth Goodwin and Al Finley just after their engagement, 1952. I was the best man at their wedding.
3. International students on a trip to Amish country, Lancaster, Pennsylvania, Christmas 1958.

Five

My First Pastorate, in New York City

Oddly enough, the beginning of my formal ministry was a call in 1959 to the pastorate of the Armenian Evangelical Church of New York City, the same church where I was ordained two years prior. I was ordained as a Congregational there, and I returned as a Presbyterian. I preached my first sermon as their pastor on September 6, 1959.

Our family made the move from Upper Darby (Philadelphia) to New York City a year after Nancy Jean, our second daughter, was born. Since we had given up on the plans to go to Syria as mission workers, we finally decided that settling into pastoral ministry was the right way to go. Since my passion was for the Armenian people, accepting a call from them was most fitting. We rented a second-floor apartment in Flushing, New York, from owners who were Greeks from Cyprus. Thus I had opportunity to practice the little Greek I still retained after years of absence from the island. On the day we moved in, while furniture was still being brought in, I looked out the window, and there on the front lawn was our four-year-old daughter, Linda, lecturing to kids from the neighborhood neatly seated in front of her. A true leader in the making!

That first parish became a real challenge and also a very rewarding ministry for me. My immediate predecessor was my cousin, the Rev. Dr. Dicran Kassouny, whose half-time ministry as pastor and half-time as practicing physician had just not worked out. He was getting burned out, while the congregation was demanding more. The pastor emeritus, Rev. Antranig Bedigian, was still very much involved in church affairs, hence a source of irritation between him and Dr. Kassouny. Here stepped in a novice new pastor! I had several vulnerabilities: my youth and inexperience, my poor grasp of the Armenian language when it came to preaching, my lack of wisdom in dealing with sensitive situations, long daily commutes from home, and a parish spread all over metropolitan New York City that I was requested to call on regularly.

The church building was an old bank in the architectural style of a Greek temple. The main floor was converted into a sanctuary, the enclosed balcony into church offices, and the basement into the fellowship hall, used for Sunday school as well. That was it. No yard, no parking spots, and no room for any expansion whatsoever. However, it was considered and held in high esteem as a "historic structure," because Rev. Bedigian had ministered there for over forty years and made quite a name for himself as a writer and scholar. Herein lay my most challenging first obstacle: How to minister in the shadow of this esteemed former pastor, and how to grow a church within such confining and restricting building facilities?

A few days after I had begun my ministry, church dignitaries came to me with a request to allow Rev. Bedigian to preach the Armenian sermon every Sunday, since my Armenian was quite poor, and also to let him edit the weekly *Tertig,* which was the official church newsletter mailed to all the households. Thus I was presented with a dilemma, in effect, to become an assistant pastor to Rev. Bedigian and work under his leadership or risk failure and rejection. My answer to them was that since I had been called to be their pastor, they should give me time to prove myself capable in all areas of ministry, including preaching in my poor Armenian; and that I would talk to Rev. Bedigian about his continuing role as pastor emeritus.

I then went to his residence in Leonia, New Jersey, and had a visit. After I acknowledged the fact that he was my mentor and highly respected senior, who had sponsored my ordination two years earlier, I presented to him a request and a proposition: I needed one year to prove my competency as a pastor, but since I could not do so unless allowed by him and the church leadership, I requested that he stay away from all church functions, including the role in the production of the *Tertig*. After one year I would include him in church functions, invite him to preach from time to time, and openly give him the honor he richly deserved. To my great surprise and relief, he agreed to do so! He passed on his decision to our elders, and the coast was clear from then on.

I spent five significant years pastoring the New York Church. Our family grew from four to six with the births of Karen Martha (November 14, 1960) and Timothy Vartkes (May 29, 1963) at North Shore Hospital in Long Island. We moved to a much bigger Dutch Colonial house in Flushing, where the children could grow and flourish. My wife, Addie, worked nights as a nurse, began to raise four great children, and provided excellent help to me in my ministry as well. She helped in teaching in our Sunday school and organized an evening women's group for young working mothers. To do this, she would drive all over New York and even cross George Washington Bridge to New Jersey to gather and return members of the group. That was no easy task. With our pooled resources, hard work, and the cooperation of the church members, the Sunday school grew significantly to over forty children. To succeed in doing so in one cramped basement hall, in downtown Manhattan, was quite an accomplishment!

In our fourth year it became quite clear to us, and a number of others, that the cramped and outdated building we were using as a church had reached its maximum capacity. Something would have to be done about it. Our Council thought long and hard about this and organized a task group to study the matter and bring a recommendation for action. When the news of this got out, it created quite a stir. Finally, Rev. Bedigian came to me to hear about our plans.

"We have a dream to move to larger quarters and grow the church without the hindrances of space and distances," I said.

"Well, let it remain a dream until I die!" he replied. With that position adopted by him, and knowing that it was supported by the old guard, I went to the Council with my decision.

"I am sorry, but I cannot continue as your pastor. With the commitment of the leaders to a building and not to the future, with young families and children, what you need here is not a young pastor with young children, but one who will maintain this place and its history."

Having served notice that I would be gone in a year, we returned to our work and ministry. It was very soon after this turn of events that we had a visitor in our church service on Sunday morning. He was Ernest Bedrosian of Fowler, California, an elder in the First Armenian Presbyterian Church of Fresno, California. He met with me following the service and proceeded to tell me that they were looking for a pastor and asked me if I'd be interested in that position. The timing was perfect, and after consulting with Addie and the children, I responded to his inquiry with a "Yes!" Thus the great adventure of our first pastorate in New York City was soon to end and a new chapter would open before us.

A number of significant events took place during my tenure in New York. In 1962, my parents, Manuel and Martha Kassouni, emigrated from Cyprus. This was monumental for me and my family. I grew up with no grandparents, but how fortunate it was going to be for my children to have a grandfather and a grandmother. Addie's parents had died before they could get to really know them. Her mother, Siroon, died from cancer in 1956, and her father Misak, died from a heart attack in 1962. My daughter, Linda, remembers him fondly, and Nancy does so faintly, but Karen and Tim do not. Unfortunately, none of them got to know Siroon. In 1964 my parents moved to Fresno, to join us after our move there. There they lived comfortably, became an integral part of our family, and were highly respected members of our church and community.

While still in New York, I was elected to be the moderator of the Armenian Evangelical Union (Eastern States and Canada). This union of several Armenian Evangelical churches had expanded to include Canada. A new worshiping fellowship in Toronto, under the leadership of Mr. Solomon Nigosian, had been meeting for some time in the Nazarene church facility there and now wished to be recognized as a member congregation. This was an exciting event, because we had not had a new church started in over fifty years. Immigrants from the Middle East were coming to Canada, because the United States was hard to enter. At that time immigration from Soviet Armenia was nonexistent. The Armenian population in the United States was assimilating into the American language and culture, and our churches were attracting very few young people. Hence, the prognosis for their future was bleak. Leaders, such as the Rev. A. A. Bedigian, were advising us to attach ourselves to existing American churches, because our churches would cease to exist before too long.

In the light of this growing viewpoint, the proposal to support the Canadian congregation seemed absurd to many. Consequently, when they applied to the AEU for $30,000 in partial support for purchasing the facility they were using, it was received with skepticism. As the moderator, I saw it otherwise and advocated for raising the support they were seeking. I approached thirty people with a request to donate $1,000 each over three years, to obtain the needed amount. We raised the money despite the refusal of several philanthropic leaders to do so because they thought it would be a waste of money. My answer to them was, "Armenians are coming to North America because their future in the Middle East is questionable. The future of Armenians, outside of Armenia, will be decided in North America." So it is what began as a modest project in Toronto that has grown to the point today where millions are being spent on Armenian churches, schools, camps, and related institutions. This is being done in partnership with the AMAA (Armenian Missionary Association of America).

Solo Nigosian came from Egypt to Toronto and began the ministry mentioned. However, he was a layman at the time. In 1963 his application to our Union for ordination was approved. He was the second person ever to be ordained in North America. The first such person, I was told, was the Rev. H. Aharonian, who was ordained a number of years earlier and had gone on to lead the Armenian Evangelical community in the Middle East. Solo's ordination was set for November 30, 1962, in his church in Toronto, which I was to lead. My father, and our lay leader, Steve Mardiguian accompanied me as I drove out of New York City on November 29, making an overnight stop in Albany, New York, to pick up the Rev. A. Goergizian.

The four of us started out early next morning in a snow storm which got worse and worse as we drove on the New York Thruway toward Buffalo. The storm turned into a blizzard, and the road condition became almost impossible. Cars, trucks, and buses were skidding off the highway and ending up in the ditches. I was really concerned, as was everyone else. We grew very quiet, afraid to say anything. Would we make it in time for the service at 7:00 p.m.? Would we make it at all?

I prayed and drove on slowly, following in the tracks of a huge eighteen wheeler. After ten grueling hours we made it to Buffalo, and then on to Niagara Falls. I had promised my dad I'd take him to see Niagara Falls. When we got there, ice had formed and piled up high as the falls kept tumbling over, and the country-side was covered deep in snow. It was a fantastic and unforgettable scene. We jumped out of the car for a quick view and jumped back in in less than five minutes before we froze to death!

I telephoned Solo with the news that we were running late and instructed him to start the service without us and promised that somehow we'd get there in time for the ordination.

From Niagara Falls the weather calmed and the blizzard stopped. After two hours we arrived at the church. They had already sung a number of hymns and were bravely carrying on and praying that we would get there safely. Thank God we did! It had taken us over twelve hours. We then proceeded to the ordination of a minister for our churches for the first time in years. We thus opened a new chapter in the life of the Armenian Evangelical community in North America.

California, Here We Come

Our family piled into our Ford Fairlane station wagon in August of 1964 and drove west, heading to our destination, Fresno, California. It took us two weeks, with stops in Jamestown, New York, to visit with my brother Sarkis and Olivette and family and sightseeing in must-see places, such as Yellowstone National Park, Wyoming. We entered California via Tioga Pass, starting at Lee Vining, an entry point for Yosemite National Park. Our desire was to go on from there to Fresno. In those days Tioga Pass was a winding two lane road climbing over nine thousand feet going up the sheer canyon. The road was not even paved then but crushed rock all the way. It was a scary trip indeed. Our one saving feature was that going up the canyon we hugged the side of the mountain. For those coming down, one missed turn meant a plunge down hundreds of feet and certain death!

Our first stop after entering California was to enjoy a picnic lunch at Tuolumne Meadows, Yosemite National Park. This idyllic setting of green fields nestled among gorgeous peaks and forests provided an ideal rest stop. We were the only people there, as far as we could see. While we were enjoying our meal in the magical quiet of nature, I began to hear faint sounds of people talking. As the sound drifted in and out, I thought I heard Armenian being spoken. I walked toward the source, and sure enough there was another family having a picnic, and they were Armenian. We encountered no other people there. Aha! This was an omen affirming my coming to pastor the First Armenian Presbyterian Church of Fresno. Welcome to California!

My Second Pastorate, Fresno

The church offered us their parsonage (called a "Manse" in Presbyterian parlance) as our home in Fresno. It was a small house of some thirteen hundred square feet with no air conditioning. We arrived there in early September in stifling heat, with the temperature over one hundred degrees, even though it was toward the end of summer. Needless to say, it was a challenge for six of us to squeeze in and enjoy our new home. However, it had several features that helped us endure one year there, before we decided we had to find our own quarters and buy our own house. One was a rather large back yard and garden. It had a big tangerine tree which produced delicious fruits and also provided our kids opportunity to try their climbing skills. Another asset was that we could plant a vegetable garden there and enjoy its produce. This we did. One item we planted was radish. This is an easy vegetable to plant and grow, and sure enough the green shoots appeared before too long. A few days later, when I came home, my daughters ran out with excited news that all the radishes had been pulled out and were lying on the ground next to where they had been planted. Well, it seems Tim was the culprit. At the age of two years his curiosity had gotten the best of him. In answer to my question as to why he had done this, he replied, "I wanted to see the roots, Daddy!" We can't find fault in that, can we?

Another good thing was that the house was only one block away from the church. Walking to church made quite a change and a treat for us, since in New York we either drove for an hour to go from Flushing to midtown Manhattan, or we had to take the subway train to get there.

We lived in the manse for two years and then moved into a larger house, mostly for the children's sake, two miles on the eastside of town. The old manse was sold for $13,000 by the church, and I was given a housing allowance over and above my $6,000 a year salary, so we could buy our own house. The price was $28,000, which was double the price for the old manse. "How could they afford it?" church folks asked. Well, Addie's dad had initially helped us, and our income was augmented by Addie working nights at the community hospital as a nurse, which she had been doing for years, and so we were able to make the move. It provided an excellent home allowing our children growth and enjoyment. The house had an old pool (actually a reservoir) with its own well. It had a big orchard with over a dozen fruit trees and several big trees for the kids to climb and use as their mystery hideouts. Every two weeks I emptied the pool into prebuilt channels to water the orchard. Before going to bed, I'd turn on the pump, and by daybreak the pool would be full again with fresh but cold water. We'd wait a day or two for the sun to warm it, and then the kids would jump in and have a great time.

Fresno is where Armenian immigrants to California settled in the early 1800s, attracted by the climate for health reasons and the fertile soil for farming. They were hardy and pious folks, whose love for God led them to the founding of the first Armenian church of any denomination in California, named the First Armenian Presbyterian Church. In 1892 the women formed a ladies' aid society, and in 1897 the church itself was organized with the help of the Presbytery of Stockton. A retired Armenian-speaking former American missionary in Turkey, the Rev. Lysander Burbank, became their first pastor. They built their first edifice in the downtown area in 1905. The renowned author William Saroyan attended there as a boy and mentions it in a number of his stories. One worth telling is that he and his friends used to sit in the balcony and gaze down at the people in worship. They counted how many men were bald, because "they were the rich ones." Now I know why I've had a full head of hair all my life!

In 1942 the church moved to a new facility on South First Street. That area, on the eastern part of town was considered a suburb then. Huntington Boulevard, across the church, was where many mansions of the rich were located. However, when I came there in 1964, the area had deteriorated, and the City of Fresno had instituted a redevelopment program. The city had bought many houses in the neighborhood and demolished them, making room for new homes to be built.

Availing themselves of the opportunity, the church bought several lots on either side and agreed to hold the open spaces for a future building program. This acquisition was central for the church's vision for growth. Confined to their existing quarters that had grown inadequate, several leaders had done the courageous thing and planned ahead. At that critical stage, I was invited to be their pastor. Attendance had dropped significantly, and they knew something had to be done. This fact was my main reason for accepting their call. It was an exciting and invigorating challenge indeed. We had a common vision: to grow again and be a vital presence for Christ in that community. My understanding was that the lay leadership would support me in this endeavor. Alas, the road to the fulfillment of our dream was much rockier than we had imagined it would be.

To Build or Not to Build

About two years after I'd begun my ministry there, I approached the Session (board of elders) and reminded them that the time to act on our intentions and realize our vision for expanded facilities had come. I also reminded them that my acceptance of their call extended to me to be their pastor was predicated on this fact.

With this challenge facing us, they began to get cold feet! Hesitation, excuses, and outright opposition arose. Some members said the existing building was good enough. Others said the membership was too small. They questioned what we would do with the existing building. Many said we could not possibly raise the amount of money needed. They also could not let go of the existing building because of many loving memories it held for them. These were some of their reasons for hesitating to forge ahead.

"Can we at least hire an architect to draw some preliminary plans and show us what we can do?" I asked. To this they finally agreed but insisted that we should get the consent of the congregation before going any further. Thus we began the uncertain journey forward. The next step was to go to the congregation with the request that we hire an architect to draw preliminary plans. When we convened the meeting again, excuses began to pour in, with threats on the part of a few that they would leave the church if we proceeded. One prominent couple actually did so, and they were the ones who lived closest.

One old-time member stood up and said, "*Badveli* (pastor), what are you going to do when the pillars of the church move away?"

"Well," I replied, "God will keep the roof from falling, when and if the pillars were to move!"

Building Young Lives

Along with our concentration on the need for new facilities, we saw early on that our young people needed special care for their own life and the growth of the church. The Sunday school, under the loving and dedicated service of Ernest Tavlian (he was a veteran of World War II, and a survivor of the Bataan death march) was holding on and needed our encouragement. This we did, and the school began to grow. We had a great group of high-school and college-age youth. Apart from the regular weekly youth programs, we instituted a weekly Tuesday Bible class, with coffee and donuts, for collegians, from 6:00 to 8:00 a.m. It was quite popular, drawing youth from beyond our church, along with our own.

In the summer of 1966, we organized a team of collegians and named it Summers for Service. The idea was to go to the Middle East and work in youth camps and conferences for several weeks, sharing their faith, witnessing to Christ, and helping out as requested. Kenneth Bedrosian, Darrell Lazarus, Harry Mickalian, and Kenneth Durkin (from Los Angeles) formed that team. They spent a week at Camp Armen, an extension of the Youth Home for Armenian children in Tuzla, near Istanbul, established by Hrant Guzelian in 1960. He had the vision and the commitment to go into the interior of Turkey and gather children of Armenian descent, who had no knowledge of their Armenian identity or Christian faith, and bring them to Istanbul. There they had converted the basement of the Armenian Evangelical Church of Gedig Pasha and literally "saved" the children from cultural and spiritual oblivion. The team provided the same kind of support in Lebanon and Syria, in centers such as Kechag (Christian Endeavor) and other summer youth conferences.

This experience had a profound influence on a number of young people. I keep coming across some of them (now adults) in my travels. Kenneth Bedrosian, a member of the team has said to me, "It was a life- and soul-changing experience for me." My only regret is that we did not continue this program, for a variety of reasons.

After five years of hard work and uphill battles to help our church find a new direction for growth and to chart new courses for its future, I was ready for a break. It came in a totally unexpected way.

Around the World in Ninety Days

The year 1969 was "a very good year" as the song made famous by Frank Sinatra has it. Out of the blue, I received an invitation from the Rev. Hagop Sagherian in Beirut, Lebanon inviting me on behalf of the Union of Armenian Evangelical Churches in the Middle East to come there for a five-week preaching mission, with one week in each of five different churches. This invitation came at a very opportune time, because I needed a sabbatical change and was getting stressed out with all the challenges facing us. The time-frame would be from October to December, with my return to Fresno in time to celebrate Christmas. After consulting with my wife, Addie, and family, and also with our Session, I accepted with deep thanks. Without the understanding and cooperation of my family I could not have gone on this mission. I have been deeply grateful for this gift to me by them all.

Summer 1969 was a special year for all of us for another reason. The first landing on the moon by US astronauts in the Apollo 11 Mission took place that year. It was a very special day for us in our home as well. On July 21, all six of us gathered in our patio room where a brand-new color television was installed (first time for us) to watch the drama unfold. In silence, but with hearts beating in excited and apprehensive expectations, we watched the capsule land. First came the famous words by Neil Armstrong, "The eagle has landed." Then when he stepped on the surface of the moon he made an unforgettable statement: "That's one small step for man, one giant leap for mankind."

We all burst out with joy and shouted excitedly, "We beat the Russians! We beat the Russians!" After the excitement had died down, and we were still together sharing our thoughts, my son Timothy (who was six years old then) came to me and whispered in my ear, "Dad, what's a Russian?"

As we all laughed out loud at the question of this innocent child, I pondered about our times of competition and the dangerous rivalry going on between the Soviet Union and our country. Since then I also have often asked myself, "What's a Russian?" This question was for me a prophetic one, finding new meaning when I was in Moscow that fall, on my way to Beirut, Lebanon.

On September 22, I began the journey by flying to London. There I visited friends from Cyprus, whom I had not seen in years. From there, I flew to Copenhagen, then to Stockholm, finally arriving in Moscow at the beginning of October. My plan was to go to Armenia for three days on my way to Beirut. However, it was mandatory for all travelers in the Soviet Union, in those days, to enter by way of Moscow, and then catch a flight beyond. Since I had to go to Moscow first, I took advantage of the opportunity and explored that magnificent city.

Traveling alone, I was very conscious of how vulnerable I was and took care in that regard. And yet I was very excited to be there and had some "must see, must do" objectives. Beyond seeing the famous sights of tombs and museums, I wanted to connect with the people.

First, I wanted to worship in a Russian Protestant church. I did that by going to the Baptist Church (all Protestants were grouped under that one umbrella identity by the government) and worshiping with them. It was an unforgettable experience. When I got there, the church was packed with hundreds of worshipers, and the aisles were full with people standing, taking up every foot of space. After realizing that I was an American, the ushers led me to the balcony and signaled for a man to get up and give me his seat! Deeply thankful for his courtesy, I listened with rapt attention as they were singing a hymn which I recognized, but not knowing Russian I could not sing with them.

I listened with my heart as the sermon was preached, and then what followed shook me to the core of my soul: the celebration of Holy Communion. After the consecration of the elements, first the bread and then the cup were handed to the elders to distribute to the congregation. But it was impossible for them to move up and down the aisles because of the press of the people. All they could do was hand it to the nearest person, who in turn passed it on to others. I watched from the balcony in utter amazement. The Holy Spirit was moving in and among them, as in the day of Pentecost!

When our turn came in the balcony, someone passed to me the sacred bread and then the cup, whispering in Russian, "the body of Christ," and then, "the blood of Christ." At that miraculous moment, I had a flashback to July 21, and my son Tim whispering in my ear, "Dad, what's a Russian?" There was no Cold War in that gathering. There was no sense of fear or alienation, only a deep sense of unity in Christ, and a celebration of his presence. As St. Paul says in Ephesians 2:14, "He (Christ) is our peace; in his flesh he has made both groups (Jews and Gentiles, and now Americans and Russians) into one, and has broken down the dividing wall, that is the hostility between us."

It is ironic that the Berlin Wall still stood then, and the hostilities between the Soviet Union and America were in full evidence. But here, there was no wall at all, and we were one in Christ! After that experience, whenever I am inclined to withdraw from people who are different from me, and I seek comfort within the walls of separation, a little voice in me says, "What's a Russian?" Empowered with that memory and that experience in the Holy Spirit, I reach out in faith and "pass the bread and the cup" to my neighbor.

I had another experience in Moscow that was precious, although not of the spiritual variety which I had in the church. I had heard that there was an Armenian restaurant there called "Ararat Restaurant." By going there it was my hope to connect with some local Armenians. There being no empty table for one, I was seated at a table with a married couple. It turned out that they were Russian. Since I spoke no Russian, and they spoke no Armenian or English, we ate in utter silence…quite the opposite of what my hopes were.

However, glancing over at other tables, I noted one with a group of men eating and drinking with obvious enjoyment and gusto. I could easily hear they were Armenian. What was noticeable was that one prominent man at their table was being approached with respect and deference. I supposed that he was recognized by all as a high-ranking politician. I kept munching my meal and glancing over to their table with great interest. Finally, I got up the nerve and walked over to them and said, "Greetings, brothers. Pardon me for intruding, but I could not resist a desire to come over after I heard you speaking Armenian. You see, I am alone, traveling from America to Armenia. My heart burned within when I heard you speaking our mother tongue. I have not heard much for years! Could I sit at your table and visit with you?"

"Welcome comrade ("*Enger*" in Armenian), welcome," greeting me with great warmth. "You of course may join. Have a seat, and have a drink with us!"

I then moved over and sat down with them, never looking back to see what my former tablemates were doing. They poured me a glass of koniak (brandy) and began to offer toasts, one after another. I dared not refuse; however, I also was very aware that I dared not lose control of my senses, because this was going to be a very interesting evening indeed. In my heart I prayed, "God, help me not to get drunk! I am all alone and have no idea how to cope if I get into trouble in Moscow!"

In answer to their questions that kept coming, as they, and especially their leaders, wanted to know who I really was, I proceeded to tell them that I was a teacher (I had received a visa under that declaration, because minister/clergy would not mean anything to them), and that I had saved money for years, dreaming of seeing our motherland, Armenia. They questioned me about life in America and about my wife and family there. Always on my guard for questions digging into any political motivations, I was asked, "What do you think of Armenians escaping Armenia through Turkey because of conditions there?"

"I am a plain and ordinary teacher," I told them. "I have no political affiliations, and I know nothing of Armenians escaping through Turkey." Again, let me remind our readers that those were the days of the Soviet Union, and Leonid Brejhnev was their president. There was no emigration out of Armenia allowed or tolerated, hence their interest in clandestine operations that were going on in that regard.

After several more drinks on their part, and careful sipping from one glass on my part, their leader said to me, "Comrade, I invite you to come with us to my house to meet my wife and my son. Come along with us. I'll call her and ask her to spread a table of food for us." The time was past ten o'clock already, and warning bells began to go off in my head. However, I dared not refuse their hospitality and proceeded to join them.

Piling into two taxis, we went to a house I know not where. They could have been kidnapping me, and I could do nothing about it. We finally arrived at our destination and walked up to an apartment that amazed me with its size and opulence. It was large and furnished with Persian rugs, television, piano, and fine furniture. Sure enough, his wife, to whom I was properly introduced, had spread a table for us. His young son was also proudly introduced. He was dressed in a Russian Cossack outfit, and when called on by his father he danced a Cossack dance for us, which he did with great pride. While I watched in silent admiration, my thoughts drifted to my home and family, and my son Timothy, of whom this boy reminded me so much.

We sat down at the table and ate and drank some more, till past midnight. The critical moment came for me when this man of obvious high standing invited me to walk around and see the rest of his apartment. When we were alone in their bedroom he asked me in a muted voice, "Do you have any gold, any gems, any diamonds to sell? I'd be glad to buy them from you if you do." Aha, that was it! With a calm and steady voice I replied, "No comrade, I told you I was a teacher with just enough money to make it to Armenia and back. I have no gold or jewelry to sell."

Satisfied with my answer, we went back to the dining room to rejoin the party. Things wound down fast after that. Close to 2:00 a.m., the man said, "It's quite late. I will call a taxi to take you to your hotel. I will pre-pay him the fare, so be sure he does not ask for any money from you." After exchanging words of deep gratitude and farewell, we proceeded back downstairs. I climbed into the taxi and went on my way to my hotel. How about that for my wish to meet with some of the locals in Moscow? Again, the thought came to me, "What's a Russian?"

From Moscow we flew to Yerevan, the capital of Armenia. Hotel Armenia was my destination. It was nothing special, and the presence of Russian domination was everywhere. The cashier at the hotel desk was Russian, and every floor had a Russian woman sitting in the hallway watching everyone going in and out. My feelings of exhilaration at finally standing in the capital of my fatherland were counterbalanced with sadness that I was there alone. This sense of aloneness had begun to grow in me, starting in Stockholm, Sweden and now hit me hard in Armenia. It was the land of my fathers, but my father was not there. It was the land of my people, but my family was not there. It was the land where my mother tongue was spoken, but their Eastern Armenian dialect (we called it Russian-Armenian) was strange and hard to understand. I was there not as a native son but as a typical tourist.

My mother had told me she had a cousin and family living there. After some searching I did connect with them. They were her sister, Marie Aylanjian and family. With great joy they welcomed me and invited me to dinner. Her daughter, Aznive, went shopping and came back after some time with the news that she finally was able to buy a chicken for our dinner. Times were tough in those Soviet era days. Her husband asked me what my profession was. I told him I was a minister. "What's that?" he asked. "Do you mean a priest?" In my response, I explained that I was not a priest, since I was Protestant (or Evangelical, as we are called in the Middle East). I told him that our beliefs and practices are people oriented, with very little liturgy, no hierarchy, and a direct approach to God in simple faith, with no other mediators except Jesus Christ. I shared the fact that the central tenet of our faith was God's love for us, demonstrated in the life, death, and resurrection of Jesus Christ.

His response was very significant, because he was typical of the people living in a communist system. "Religion is not for me," he said. "It is for children and old people but not for thinking people or adults.

Children need the pageantry and excitement of times like Christmas, and the old need it to prepare themselves for death." However, after I explained more about how we are people oriented and services for the poor and the needy is a prime focus of our purpose, he replied, "You know, I could be Protestant!"

I had also heard that my father's sister Vartouhi, who died in child-birth, had a son who survived and went to Armenia from Aleppo after World War II. Evidently, the news about me had got around, and on the last day (I was there only three days), a man came to the hotel and looked me up. He was Vartouhi's son Garbis Demirdjian. He was distraught that I was leaving soon, and that all he could do was give me a gift for my father, a bottle of Armenian koniak. I carried it all the way around the world and back to America and gave it to my father. After he died, I found it unopened in his kitchen. I took it from there and still have it in our house today.

One cannot but marvel at how this ancient people have maintained their heritage, rooted in Christianity. They have hung on with great pride and survived great onslaughts of invaders but never let go of their souls. Rooted, like ancient trees, they have clung to the very rocks, of which there is plenty.

The saying goes that after God created the world, God had a lot of rocks left over. There was still one people left to situate in their country, the Armenians.

So God said, "Sorry, all I have left for you is a pile of rocks."

"We'll take it!" they replied.

With those rocks they built magnificent churches and monasteries. Their center, Holy Etchmiadzin, (meaning, the descent of the Only Begotten) is the cathedral a few miles from Yerevan, which their Catholicos (the universal head of the Armenian church), St. Gregory the Illuminator, built in the fourth century AD. I took a guided tour to see all I could in the short time I had, and I visited a number of these ancient churches. One that stuck in my memory as a symbol of their faith and their tenacity was the Monastery of Keghart. The whole church edifice was carved out of rock and was not visible to those outside. It was built so they could hide in this subterrainian sanctuary when invaders attacked, which they often did.

In another church, our guide took us inside and proceeded to tell the story of how Armenians adopted Christianity. Since there was nothing new there for me, I left the group and went out to the courtyard. There were two old men there, smoking their cigarettes. Around the periphery of the yard were several buildings (similar to Christian Education units in America), and children were playing there. They were all wearing the red scarves of the Communist Youth organization. So, I ambled over to these men and asked a question. "Our guide is telling the story of our Christian beginnings to the tourists inside. It is a wonderful story. Tell me, does anyone gather these children and tell them the same story of our Christian faith?"

"Of course they do," one of them answered.

"Don't believe it," said the other. "There is no such thing taught in schools here."

There you have it: the dilemma of holding on to the Christian faith on the one hand and being ruled by a godless political system on the other. No wonder that Armenia was the first republic within the Soviet system to declare independence when the USSR (Union of Soviet Socialist Republics) imploded.

The focus of my sabbatical was Beirut, Lebanon. I arrived there in the latter part of October and carried on my mission till the end of November. The Rev. Hagop Sagherian met me and drove me to his home and introduced me to his wife. I was their guest much of the time. My mission would take me to five Armenian Evangelical churches, where I would preach every evening for a week. Now, this was a big challenge for me because my Armenian was weak. However, I somehow did it, with God's help and the encouragement of my colleagues in ministry. Interest and attendance was high. It was a time of high anxiety, with the political situation in Beirut quite fragile. The people in attendance were there to find reassurance in their faith and encouragement from one who had come from America for a mission among them. One week I moved in with the Rev. Soghomom Nuyujukian, pastor of the First Armenian Evangelical Church of Beirut. Unease had settled on everyone because political friction and outright violence had broken out. Gunfire and explosions could be heard in the city. We were grounded that week and could not leave the house because of an emergency declared by the government. The political divide between Christian and Muslim factions had been slowly building in intensity and eventually, in 1976, a devastating civil war broke out and lasted for sixteen years.

Along with preaching in the evenings, I was also invited to speak on the radio for the Armenian language program. I chose as my theme 2 Timothy 1:6–7: ”I remind you to rekindle the gift of God that is within you through the laying on of my hands; for God did not give us a spirit of fear ('cowardice' RSV), but rather a spirit of power and of love and of self-control ('self-discipline' RSV).” I did so intentionally as I sought to encourage them to stand firm in the midst of emerging chaos. I did not see my role to be that of an evangelist, which I do believe was Rev. Sagherian's hope. Rather, my mission was that of a brother coming alongside (Greek: "*paraclete*") them to assure them that they were not alone, but our prayers and our support were there for them. This is the term Jesus used when he talked of the ministry of the Holy Spirit, who was to come to them after his departure from earth. The word "paraclete" is composed of two words: "*Para*" meaning alongside, and "*clete*" from the verb "to call" or "called," (e.g., paramedic). It is a beautiful word which in essence describes our role and mission in Christ's name in coming to the aid of the oppressed and needy.

I also spoke at the Armenian Christian Endeavor Youth Center called KECHAG (mentioned earlier in our trip there in 1952). It is a lovely conference center several miles away from Beirut, in the hills, built with the love and sacrificial giving of their community. Five years after I was there, it was taken over by Syrian troops who had intervened in the civil war, and they did not have it returned to them till twenty years later.

While in Beirut I had the joyful opportunity to meet some of my relatives, whom I had never met before. Among them was Dr. Yervant Kassouny, my uncle Yeghia's grandson. He and his family composed of his wife, Jeanette, and son Dicran lived in an apartment close to Haigazian College, where he was the head of the Armenian Studies Department. He is a published author, with many books written concerning Armenian history and biographies of key individuals. He is the author of the biography of my father, referred to earlier. Dr. Kassouny was for many years the editor of *CHANASSER* (The magazine of the Christian Endeavor organization in Lebanon, and an important Armenian Evangelical organ in the Middle East). He is, in my opinion, the outstanding Armenologist in our Evangelical community worldwide. Jeanette and Dicran now live in California, while Yervant continues in Beirut. We have developed a close association and stay in touch concerning publications, developments in church and society, and our literary pursuits of mutual interest.

Among other relatives I met there were my cousins from my mother's side, the Meykhanejians. Their mother, Aznive, was my mother's niece and had a very close resemblance to her. Her daughters, Lucy, Ann, and Asdghig, and sons Garabed and Hagop were all still living at home then. While there I also met another cousin, Marie Yedikian, who was attending the American University of Beirut. She was the daughter of my mother's other niece, Sirvart Yedikian, residing in Aleppo, Syria. With the onset of civil war they managed to leave under very dangerous circumstances. Aznive, Asdghig and Hagop came to California, via Cyprus, and established residency in Irvine. Years later I connected with Marie, her husband Hrant Ajamian, and family, and her parents Hovsep and Sirvart Yedikian, residing in Rancho Palos Verdes and Torrance. Her father passed away in 2007, and her husband Hrant in May of 2017, after a long struggle with cancer. Aznive passed away at the age of 92 years in November of 2016. My regret is that due to the separation of time, distances, and life's circumstances my family of relatives and I have failed to maintain closer relationships.

My father's brother Manasseh had two sons. The elder son Loutfi and his wife Marie had three children: Hovsep (wife Kelly), Manuel (fiancée Gabriela), and Zohrab (wife Laura). The younger son Edward and his wife Arax also had three children: Raffi (wife Anahid), Houri (husband Raffi Paloulian), and Vicken (wife Roumina). I had initially met Ed and Arax in Beirut. Both sons and their families immigrated to California in the early 1980s. With our support they established themselves in Los Angeles. Of special note in this regard was Ed's resolve to start a plumbing business; however, he did not speak English. I volunteered to lead him step by step, translating the official manual needed for him to pass the qualifying exam. Within a few weeks he had it down pat, and passed at the first try. He went on to establish a very successful business in Glendale.

My journey eastward from Lebanon took me next to Tehran, Iran. I stayed for three nights at the home of Rev. Nerses and Mrs. Gulenia Khachadourian, who were serving as the shepherds of the local Evangelical church. I had met them several years earlier in Syria. They had wondered if I could take over the position of director of Action Chretienne, an evangelism and service ministry with French origins in Aleppo. However, I had gone on to seminary in New York and could not take up that position.

The Shah was still in power then, and the city was open to western travelers. My lasting impression of the city was its Central Bank of Iran and the Treasury of the National Jewels. The Peacock Throne of solid gold and multiple jewels, the crowns of royalty, and buckets of diamonds on display were a sight to behold. I've seen the crown jewels in London, but they compare poorly with what this exhibit included.

My journey continued on to Calcutta, India. There I visited the historic Armenian Apostolic Church and the Armenian Academy, which had for many years been the center of the community's life. The history of Armenians in India is noteworthy. They were among traders who came from Europe, via the "silk road" originally, and then by sea, and were prominent as the primary merchants of laundry bluing. I visited their cemetery and read on the tombstones the names of their people going back over a century.

I was invited to the home of their local priest to have dinner there. During our conversation, the priest's wife, upon hearing that I was from Cyprus, asked me who were my parents. After hearing my response she exclaimed, "*Aman? Toon bedelik Vartkesen yes?*" Meaning, "Oh my! Are you the little Vartkes?"

She was the redhead daughter of the Kassabians, owners of our local Larnaca bakery where the delicious Lahmajoun (like a small pizza) was baked. As they say, "It's a small world!" Calcutta was an amazing city. What really caught my attention was that in the evening, after sunset, I smelled intense smoke of wood burning. I looked out and saw a cloud of smoke hanging around. I turned to my hosts and said, "There must be a big fire in town."

"Oh no," they replied. "The homeless who live in the streets pull out their sleeping rolls, fire up their woodburning stoves, and prepare their meals as soon as the sun sets."

"How many are they?" I asked, with my curiosity aroused.

"A million of them," they answered, to my amazement.

A million homeless in a city of seven million people! Then I remembered that Mother Teresa had her famous mission in that city, and now I understood why.

Later, I walked around for a while and watched these poor people living on the sidewalks. It boggled my mind and to this day I can't get over it. Day after day, year after year, millions upon millions of people just in that one city, let alone the hundreds of metropolises, all over the world in similar straits! It is noteworthy that the streets of downtown Los Angeles have now become shelters for hundreds of homeless also.

Some of my time was spent as a typical American tourist, flying to Agra, for example, to visit the famous Taj Mahal and to take in their amazing history. From India I flew on to Bangkok, Thailand, where I spoke at a Chinese Baptist church, and then on to the Philippines. It was a quick trip to a Bible Institute several miles outside Manila to speak and to observe another mission project affiliated with my hosts, the Christian Nationals' Evangelism Commission (CNEC). My next stop was Hong Kong and Kowloon (the mainland). I stayed there for a week and had the delightful experience of living with the local Chinese Christians and eating every meal with them during that time. Their objective was to have me experience their way of life, their food, and their faith. It was not easy eating with chopsticks, and they would not let me have a fork. It was either use chopsticks or starve!

There I visited and spoke in several Christian schools, also affiliated with CNEC. The amazing thing about them was that their playgrounds were on the rooftops of the multistory apartment buildings whose top several floors were used for the schools. Land being extremely scarce there, they had to use such innovative ways to address their educational needs. The year 1969 being a time when China was still a closed country, I could not enter it. The closest I came to it was when I was driven to the border and given a peek through binoculars. In Hong Kong I looked up a college mate from Bob Jones University, Bill Kincaid, who had a mission to the boat people there. His unusual church was on a floating barge. It was there that I was invited to speak and to celebrate Holy Communion with them.

The only country where I was a typical American tourist was Japan. I stopped there for three days, on my way back to America. In Tokyo, I visited the Union Protestant Church but did not have the opportunity to worship with them. Walking the streets of that fantastic city, I came across a big demonstration. I could tell they were communists, waving red flags and wearing red headbands. Upon my inquiring what all the shouting was about, I was told they were demonstrating against the peace treaty imposed on Japan by the United States following the Second World War. Spectators, including me, were ushered out of their way in case things got a little violent. As the saying goes, "Now, I've seen everything."

Back Home Again

I returned to the United States in time to celebrate Christmas with my family. As the plane landed in Fresno, I was met not only by a jubilant wife and children but also by Ron Karabian with a message: "Happy to see you return, *Badveli* (pastor). We need you back at church right away, because there is a move to replace you as pastor with the interim." His name was Rev. Mel Moomjean, whom I had requested to take over as interim pastor in my absence.

"Don't worry, Ron," I said. "Nothing like that will happen." And nothing did, because the replacement of a pastor in the Presbyterian Church isn't that easily done without the congregation's and presbytery's approval. What had happened was that a key family in the church, who were related to Rev. Moomjean, were expressing some wishful thinking rather loudly and scared others into thinking there was a conspiracy against me.

After three long and arduous months, I was back home ready to continue where I had left off. They were very significant months in terms of my ministry and its place within the framework of God's universal Church. First, it was extremely meaningful to me that in every city I visited, starting with Copenhagen and ending with Hong Kong, I participated in the celebration of Holy Communion with people who were total strangers to me but who became my brothers and sisters in Christ around the Holy Table. Second, that people I served taught me much more than I could ever do. Their love, their dedication, their sacrificial giving of themselves, and their hope for a future centered in Christ and not for any national or material benefits were humbling for me to see. My ministry gained a global perspective from then on and shaped the dimensions of my life in the service of Christ.

Coming back to home and family was priceless. I was profoundly grateful for my wife, Addie, who held the fort while I was gone and helped the children through those long days and weeks of having no father at home. When I walked in our house, I saw a wall of the family room covered with postcards I had sent from every city I had stopped in. It was quite a geography lesson for them. So, we regrouped and set ourselves to the task ahead of us.

A Time to Build

The most important task at hand for us to address at the church was that of the new church building program. After days of prayerful planning, a preliminary action-plan was approved and Edward Avedisian, a well-known local architect, was chosen for the task. He presented to us a beautiful three-phase plan: first, a Christian Education facility; second, a new sanctuary; and third (after the existing building was removed) a fellowship hall. I challenged the Session to go ahead and proceed with the building of the Christian Education facility on the land they had bought still sitting empty next to the existing church facility. The estimated cost for it was $225,000.

"Let's begin a three-year funding program and start raising the funds necessary," I requested.

"I know this congregation. We cannot raise more than $100,000 in that time frame," said a prominent member, who himself was quite wealthy.

Eventually, the Session and the congregation approved our plan, and we proceeded to implement phase I. The person I knew would do the job as our fund raiser was one of our own, Ronald Karabian, a very successful insurance salesman with New York Life. I went to him and prayerfully asked him to take on this challenge. To my great relief, he accepted, and so we moved forward.

I knew that for the plan to succeed, we needed at least one advance pledge of a tenth of the total $300,000 fund. I went to Mary Enoch, a leading member who had, with her then-deceased husband, donated the land on which the existing facility stood, and I boldly requested that she be our benefactor. To my great joy, she accepted. Having gained her support, I knew others who were skeptical and hesitant would follow her initiative.

Not only did we raise the funds necessary, but by 1972 when the facility was built, we had fully paid for it. The momentum that this action produced carried us all the way, and by 1976 even the new sanctuary was built with the cost of $500,000. One-third of it was paid off, and for the rest we secured a loan from the bank. The first building, completed in 1972, housed the Christian Education ministries. We could finally leave our old cramped quarters and accommodate the many children and adults in our church.

Several months after we moved in, we had a request from neighborhood folks to allow them to house a private high school for youth who had not been able to continue in the public school system, including continuation schools. After a tough time debating the request in our Session to allow it, permission was granted. That arrangement lasted for a year, but we have some interesting stories emanating from that year. One morning their principal came with a strange request: a student had brought his pet snake to the classroom, but it had slithered through a separation between a built-in closet and the wall behind, and they could not retrieve it. Playing the hero, I offered to try to get it, with strict instructions not to call the TV station about it. Well, I had to pry the closet loose. Getting on my hands and knees I reached in hoping I could get the snake, which I did. However, somebody had called the TV station after all, and they got there in time to get a beautiful photo of my behind, on my hands and knees! Sure enough, the story was on the six o'clock news. Within minutes the phone started ringing with our people wondering what in the world was going on. Needless to say, I was on the hot seat for several days after that incident.

The permission granted to this school was furthering our church's mission and commitment to the community, assuring them we were there for them as well as our own congregation. We invited Calvin Crest Conference Center (the summer camp of our presbytery) to house their office for fund-raising in our old sanctuary office, and then we provided a room for the stated clerk of the presbytery there as well. Our old fellowship hall became a hub of activity for the Fresno Metro Ministry,

Fresno Area Council of Churches, and related gatherings. I am proud to say that in turn the community took care of us. We had no vandalism, no graffiti, and no destructive act perpetrated. We were paid a very high compliment by a community leader who said,

"Pastor Kassouni, you and your church have changed the negative image of Armenians in Fresno, held by many people."

"And what is that?" I asked.

"The perception is that they are wealthy and care only for their own people and causes."

I am glad to say that not because of what we did but because of the generosity of many people, the reputation of the Armenians in Fresno has changed. Many civic leaders, teachers, judges, and college and university benefactors have come from the Armenian community there.

We also participated in community-wide efforts to address the problem of hunger in the Fresno area. For example, we helped maintain a Fresno area food pantry located in the Catholic Social Service Center. I was for two years chair of the interchurch committee that collected food from over fifty churches, supporting this pantry.

The new sanctuary building was designed by Mr. Edward Avedisian, a well-known and admired local architect. He and I met often to discuss our history, our theology, and our approach to worship, and our liturgical tradition. More importantly, how we could bring together in one building the double heritage we had inherited and the witness to it, which we sought to maintain. One from our Armenian heritage and the other from our Presbyterian history, as well as our needs for adequate space anticipating our growth.

This was phase II of our building program, which was begun in 1975. The building is unique, in that it not only reflects traditional Armenian Church architecture but also combines modern lines, clearly pointing us to the future. It is hexagonal in shape. The walls are covered with natural redwood, from where six huge curved glulam beams sweep up to the ceiling, holding the cupola at their apex. From there light comes streaming down to the Communion Table intentionally placed at the sanctuary's geometric center to draw attention to the Eucharist as the focal point in worship. Hanging from the ceiling right over the Table is a huge cross. Those who enter the sanctuary are awed, drawn in by this striking feature, aided by the huge beams, like hands held together in prayer.

There are eight faceted glass windows in the nave, with four windows in the east wall and four windows in the west wall, all organized around the theme of God revealed in Christ, from his birth to death, resurrection, and eternity. Each window has two panels, the top one depicting the story of Christ, and the bottom one the story of the Armenians, as shaped by the impact of the Gospel in forming their identity. The second flows from the first, like in an hour glass, surrounded by art work reminiscent of ancient Armenian manuscript paintings. These unique and beautiful windows are certainly worth seeing, if one were ever to visit Fresno.

Quoting from an article I wrote about this sanctuary on the occasion of its dedication, I said, "A final note needs to be made. One will realize after careful observation and concentration that in the nave itself, where worship takes place, there is no attempt to represent in picture form the person or face of God: neither the Father nor the Son. This is by design, so that one's concept of God will not be limited to humans' finite view or idea of Him. God is beyond description, beyond man's ability to contain, and eternal mystery covers Him. The Gospel affirm that no one has ever seen God. All we can do is cover our faces and cry, 'HOLY, HOLY, HOLY is the God of hosts!' Jesus said, 'God is Spirit, and those who worship Him must worship in spirit and in truth.' This is our aim, this is our aspiration. May our worship be of the heart, acceptable to God who continues to hold us in His hand." (With my apologies for not being gender sensitive relative to God in those days.)

I include this quote because my theological convictions are based in it. Religions today too glibly "contain God" in their views and oppose all others who do not conform to their image, or concept, of God. Yes, God has no gender, nor is God of any one race, nor speaks our language exclusively.

The Cummings Studios in San Rafael manufactured the glass, and they used the artistic talents of Hilda Sachs to create the art work. She took on this task with special interest, because she was a survivor of the Jewish Holocaust, and she saw in the story of the Armenians, and their suffering, a reflection of her own people's story. Bill Cummings, the owner of the Studio, is quoted as saying, "Hilda Sachs is one of this country's most distinguished creators of stained glass windows and mosaics." (*Daily Independent Journal*, San Rafael. July 8, 1972)

The two front entries into the sanctuary have each a floor-to–ceiling window, with an art wall in between, over ten feet in height. One depicts St. Mesrop Mashdots, the creator of the Armenian alphabet in the fifth century AD. The first book written in Armenian was the Book of Proverbs. So it is that the first verse from there was included in this window: "To learn wisdom and instruction, to understand words of insight." The other window depicts Jesus Christ the Lord with the first sentence from the Lord's Prayer: "Our Father which art in heaven." Between these two Narthex windows are two art walls, made of fired clay, one on the exterior side and the other on the interior. The outside wall has the ancient Armenian cross, surrounded by a variety of reproductions of bas-relief designs of decorative symbols on ancient churches in Armenia. In the interior side, it has the seal of the United Presbyterian Church surrounded by symbols, including various crosses, the dove, the burning bush, flames of fire, and the fish, signifying the earliest doctrinal confession of Christ, as God's Son, our Savior, and the triangle with an eye in the middle, signifying the Trinity. The studios of Hans Sumpf and Co. of Madera, California were the creators of this unique wall.

On April 25, 1976, the dedication of the cornerstone took place. Beneath it a time capsule was placed, including a number of significant items and "*A Message to Future Members of This Church and Its Inheritors*":

"In Fresno we have found acceptance, honor and opportunity. We have done our best to be citizens loyal to their land of adoption, and we have served zealously in times of peace and times of war. In forming this

congregation we have joined by many people who are not necessarily of Armenian heritage but are our brothers and sisters in the love of God. We bear a common confession of faith in Christ as our Lord and Savior, and we work together as one in maintaining the life of the church we love. In this community of faith we affirm each other as members of the one Body of Christ and reach out in mission to a world beyond ourselves with the liberating Gospel of Jesus Christ."

The sanctuary was dedicated on Sunday, June 13, 1976.

Renewal of the congregation went hand in hand with the renewal of our building facilities. We made a significant turnaround from being a failing and disheartened congregation to a hope-filled and enthusiastic congregation, growing in number and in spiritual vitality. Our membership grew to over three hundred, and our Sunday school flourished. We experienced joy, laughter, and an effervescence not known before. Three elements necessary for a healthy congregation fell into place: spiritual vitality, adequate building facilities, and outward-looking mission for service.

Cooperation and Action

Service in the community at large included cooperative inter-Armenian church projects. Annual participation in coming together to celebrate our national special days was a given. There were other special times worth noting. One was when we all agreed that the celebration of our inter-church gathering would take place in our new sanctuary. We agreed on doing something quite unusual: to have Father Kourken Yaralian, pastor of the Holy Trinity Armenian Apostolic Church celebrate their Mass in our sanctuary, with incense and all. And so he did. The day before, he drove up in a station wagon and brought all the necessary altar accessories and vestments. We were very close friends, so I could joke with him. "Father Kourken. Do you mean to tell me that before the Apostle Paul could celebrate Holy Communion, he brought all these items with him.

If so, how could he do it when he walked from city to city?" It was a back-handed way of saying "Our simplified way of doing it is the better way."

It was a noteworthy and memorable event. However, we had some side effects that we did not anticipate. One was the criticism Father Kourken received from his parishioners for daring to celebrate Mass in a Protestant church. The other, on a much lighter note was a little girl in church who said, "Oh, what is that smell in here?" (referring to the incense used the day before).

"Don't worry dear," I said. "We'll turn on the fans and it will be gone soon."

On April 24, 1975, we organized a solemn walk from our church to city hall (a distance of about a mile) to commemorate publicly the sixtieth anniversary of the Armenian Genocide. Several hundred people from the Armenian community showed up. Father Kourken, dressed in his clerical robe and holding a cross, led the walk. I walked alongside him dressed in my clerical robe and holding an old New Testament dating back to the early 1800s. The symbolism was clear: He represented the liturgical approach to our faith, and I represented the evangelical, Gospel-centered approach.

One other community-wide project I personally got involved in was an agreement to commission a sculptor by the name of Varaz Samuelian to create a statue of one of our legendary heroes, David of Sassoon. He was a recent immigrant from Armenia, and his style was impressionist. The two and a half ton copper statue was quite dramatic: David, on his horse, charging ahead with his sword drawn in his right hand and waving the torch of freedom in his left hand. It was met with much praise, and some derision. However, the City of Fresno did accept it, and it was erected on the courthouse grounds, where it stands to this day. I wrote the text of the statement written on a brass plaque attached to the pedestal (with apologies for not having it in gender-inclusive text. It was in 1974):

David of Sassoon is the legendary folk-hero of the Armenians, who rid their land of the foreign conquerors single handedly. It is an epic based on historical events dating back to the 7th Century A.D. Troubadours, poets and sculptors have immortalized him, for it gives eloquent expression of man's undying love of freedom. This statue represents a thousand Davids in a thousand lands where throughout all of history man has sought to sustain his freedom against overwhelming odds.

The base on which the statue stands has been designed by Varaz Samuelian, the sculptor, to tell the story of the Armenian lands and people. It depicts their alphabet, their churches, their art and culture, and their history, which dates back to 782 B.C. when the capital city of Yerevan was founded.

This gift from the Armenians to the County of Fresno is made with their profound gratitude for this land which received them in their darkest hours, and provided them with the opportunity to be reborn.

—David of Sassoon Association

From time to time, I have dabbled in poetry. One such occasion was the erection of the David of Sassoon sculpture. Until now I have not had the courage to share it with others. To include it in my memoirs seems the proper time to do so:

David of Sassoon

The will to live, the will to breathe,
To work, to love, to laugh, to sing
With hearts aflame for lands oppressed.
To dream of days gone by...
    Ah, that sweet, sweet, breath of life,
    That swells the breast, and quickens pulse,
    When slave in desperation cries,
    It is enough! We shall be free!
With nerves of steel he lights his torch,
And swings that magic sword of wrath,
Until the heel of foreign hordes
Lies silent in the dust!

Breathe deep, you sons of thunder.
Your land is free again!
Sing out, you daughters of wonder,
Your honor now reclaim!

Varaz Samuelian's home and studio were near our church in downtown Fresno. From time to time, I used to drop in on him and chat about his sculptures. One other person who used to do that was the renowned author William Saroyan. This was in the same part of town where our old church building used to be and also where he grew up. Mr. Saroyan would ride his bicycle all over town from his residence in West Fresno. There were times when he came by my office, during our new building in progress, and we'd chat about our plans and his opinions. He heard me speak on the radio once (it was a five-minute midnight meditation), and he made it a point to compliment me about it. That's the closest I ever got to discussing with him his opinions and his views on matters spiritual.

In 1972, while still in Fresno, I was invited by Dr. John Hanessian Jr. to join the National Steering Committee of the Armenian Assembly of America, which was still in its infancy. He and Dr. Haikaz Grigorian, both of George Washington University, had the initial dream to start this new organization. The vision was to bring all Armenian organizations into a cooperative and nonpartisan effort and to have a united front relative to the Congress of the United States and the American public, concerning the causes which we all upheld.

I did accept this invitation and for a year made several trips to Washington, DC, to attend their meetings. It is noteworthy that we stayed at the Howard Johnson Hotel, right across from the Watergate complex made famous by the break-in to the national offices of the Democratic National Committee. This event led to the eventual resignation of President Richard Nixon. In the room where I stayed while there, my attention was caught by the policies of the hotel posted on the inside of the entry door. Added to the usual list of items was a hand written note: "And no spying allowed!" That was the room, or one like it, used by the spies when they took photos of the comings and goings of the Democratic National Committee people.

The purpose of our committee was to take charge of the assembly's business on an interim basis and prepare the way for the appointment of a board of directors in the near future. My association with the assembly provided the incentive to gather key people back in Fresno and form a group who would devote themselves to similar intercommunity efforts. At first my membership in the committee did not sit very well with several other members because I was clergy and Protestant, and there were no Apostolic clergy members. Membership in the steering committee included a number of luminaries of the Armenian community at large. Among these were Hrair Hovnanian, Cofounder of Hovnanian Construction Co; Avedis Sanjian, professor at UCLA; Lionel Galstaun, industrialist from San Francisco; Robert Kaloosdian Esq., lawyer from Boston; Stephen Mugar, owner of Star Markets; Hagop Nersoyan, theologian and author; Dennis Papazian, professor at University of Michigan.

In the Fresno area, several people joined me in organizing local support for the Armenian's assembly and promoting worthy causes, such as the observance of the Armenian Genocide. Key people in this regard were Dr. Arthur Margosian, professor at Cal State University, Fresno, and editor of the *Armenian Courier*; Allan Jendian, deacon at St. Paul Armenian Apostolic Church; Jane Bedrosian (Mrs. Kenneth Bedrosian) the administrative assistant of First Armenian Presbyterian Church; and Gilbert Khachadourian, head of the Social Security Administration in Central California.

Unfortunately Dr. Hanessian died prematurely in the crash of a Turkish Airlines DC10 (how ironic). However, since its inception the Armenian Assembly has grown dramatically and is widely recognized as the leader in Armenian-American related issues and concerns regarding the Armenian people and the American government and public at large.

A New Union is Born

In 1971, that which had been a dream for many of us finally materialized. It was the merger of two Armenian Evangelical unions into one union, covering the whole continent of North America. Previous to that we had an Armenian Evangelical Union of Eastern States and Canada, and an Armenian Evangelical Union of California. What had kept them apart was geographical separation, not ideology or theology. Crossing the continent used to be a rare experience. However, travel had become much more frequent in the '60s. Personal travels were bringing families and people together so often that increasingly talk of merger was on the minds of many. Several of us came together and drafted a plan for it. These were the Rev. Harry Missirlian, pastor of Pilgrim Armenian Congregational Church of Fresno; Rev. Vartan Hartunian, pastor of First Armenian Church, Belmont, Massachusetts; Rev. Dr. Giragos Chopourian, executive director of the AMAA, Paramus, New Jersey; Rev. Dr. Vahan Tootkian, pastor of the Armenian Congregational Church of Detroit, Michigan; and myself. At that time I was in Fresno, California.

After broaching the idea to others and bringing it up at the annual meetings of the respective unions, agreement was received. We worked on a set of guidelines, and a general plan was developed. The first meeting of the merged unions, called the Constitutional Assembly, took place in the Detroit church (actually in Southfield, a suburb). The pastor, the Rev. Dr. Vahan Tootikian, was our gracious host. He has continued to hold a significant position of leadership, both in the AEUNA (Armenian Evangelical Union of North America) and in the AMAA (Armenian Missionary Association). He is a prolific writer, historian, and an advocate for Armenian Evangelicalism worldwide. After his retirement as pastor, he assumed the position of executive director of the World Armenian Evangelical Council. It is a loose federation of seven unions: Near East (UAECNE, Lebanon, and Syria), Armenia, France, Eurasia, Europe (a fellowship), and the United States.

The first moderator of the new union was the Rev. Harry Missirlian of Fresno. We worked closely with each other and organized the first General Assembly to take place at Pacific College, Fresno, California, in 1972. I volunteered to prepare and publish our quarterly organ called the *Armenian Evangelical Outlook*. Until then the *Outlook* was a joint venture with the AMAA. That plan did not work because AMAA needed a regularly published magazine. However, regularity of publication was not kept, making Dr. Chopourian (the AMAA Director) very unhappy. So it is that we agreed to have each organization publish their own organ. Jim Aaron, a member of our church, agreed to design the masthead, which was in use for a number of years. In 1980, I was elected moderator of AEUNA and served till 1982.

Concurrent with the formation of the union, we adopted a plan to bring in needed funds. A million-dollar campaign was started with the Rev. Vartan Hartunian as the fund-raiser. Doing this was something new for our churches, because only the AMAA had been the recipient of mission giving before. Consequently, to eliminate any sense of competition, the AMAA and the AEUNA leadership came together, and a plan was adopted. The AMAA agreed to provide the necessary funds for church development, and the AEUNA agreed to cease their aggressive fundraising. A Joint Home-Missions committee was formed to implement funding of mutually acceptable projects.

In 1978, the respective youth organizations affiliated with the two unions finally agreed to merge and become one youth federation called the Armenian Evangelical Youth Fellowship (AEYF). The merger was formalized at the General Assembly meeting at Haverford College, Haverford PA. Before that, Rev. Dr. Chopourian and I met often to discuss the emergence of this youth program and put down in writing relevant ideas. Consequently we ended up writing what eventually became their initial by-laws. This youth organization has continued to grow, bringing scores of youth together. Every two years the youth organization (AEYF) and the church delegates (AEUNA) convene their General Assembly and meet concurrently.

Struggles with Social Witness

Getting involved in the area of our social witness beyond the local church was quite a challenge. Tension between the local church and its needs versus the global mission of the church always exists. My conviction has always been that we must look beyond our walls and our membership, to our calling to "go into the whole world." One day as I was sharing this challenge we faced at FAPC, one of our dear, and very wealthy, women said,

"*Badveli*, charity begins at home."

"How old is our church?" I asked.

"Seventy five," she answered.

"Very well then," I responded. "Charity has already begun here, and it's time we enlarged our horizons and reached out into the world. There is a saying which I believe is very true: 'Charity begins at home, but if it ends there, it ends.'"

The perennial issue splitting the PC(USA) Church was the issue of evangelism vs. social witness. So-called conservatives were aligned against so-called liberals, and the debates continued ad infinitum. It was especially so in California. Central to my involvement in that sphere was my being willing to take an active role in the Presbytery of San Joaquin (in which our church was a member). When we first moved to Fresno, the Rev. Bob Oerter, pastor of First Presbyterian Church, told me, "Kass, we need your participation and your leadership in this presbytery. First Armenian Presbyterian Church has sought our support in the past only when they had internal disputes and struggles. We need your church's participation in the community at large." Consequently I became very active in San Joaquin Presbytery, serving them as moderator, and then as chair of the Social Ministries committee.

From time to time, I was invited to speak in churches of our presbytery. For example, in 1973, the Rev. Bill Charlton, pastor of our Presbyterian church in Ridgecrest extended an invitation to me to lead a morning Bible study for adults in his church. Ridgecrest is in China Lake, on the Eastern side of California, close to Nevada, where the US

Navy has a huge base. I chose the Old Testament prophecy of Habakkuk, centering on the theme of the book, "The righteous live by their faith" (Hab. 4:4). This gem of a book has much for us who wonder why God does not intervene when innocent people suffer.

On my return to Fresno from Ridgecrest, I decided not to take the freeways but use Highways 178, 155, and 190, which were the slower routes going through the Sierras. One reason I did that was to enjoy my new car, a Datsun 240Z, driving on mountain roads. The other reason is that I have a natural inclination to use the roads less travelled and explore and discover new places.

I call the desire of most people to use the shortest and fastest routes "freeway mentality." In this case, as I was driving up into the mountains, I kept seeing signs to Cathedral Rocks. From the valley below I kept coming closer and closer to these magnificent cliffs, and they did resemble cathedrals. At the top of the mountain, there was a sign pointing to the entrance to the Cathedral Rocks Park. I immediately pulled in and parked my car. Then I walked up to the very top of these cliffs to take in the magnificent panoramas of the valleys below. I encountered no other cars or persons and was completely alone. I sat down on a rock with the magnificent view of the valley below. In total silence, I lapsed into deep meditation. When I refocused my attention on my surroundings, I saw something most unusual. Right next to me, I saw a bunch of fresh black grapes! The stem was green and the berries plump and not wilted. I looked around, but there was no other person there, and I don't remember seeing it before I sat down.

What was this? I had not eaten since I left Ridgecrest, and there were no stores for me to buy lunch. I then had a very awe-filled moment as I remembered the prophet Elijah, and how he was fed by ravens in the mountains of the Sinai desert. Was God feeding me also?

I took the grapes but would not eat any, in case someone was playing a game of some sort and had the grapes laced with some psychedelic drug. I left the park and drove until I saw a mountain stream along the road. I washed the grapes in ice-cold water, and after giving thanks I had a very hearty lunch! This incident stands out in my memory as one of the most awe-inspiring experiences I've ever had.

In the mid-1970s, the most critical and controversial issue we faced in the San Joaquin Valley was the boycotting of table grapes by the Farm Workers Organizing Committee, led by Cesar Chavez and centered in Delano, California, a few miles north of Bakersfield. Over several years, they had tried to bargain with the growers, with little to show for their efforts. Their issues dealt with low wages, very poor housing for migrant workers, and poor working conditions in the fields. First, they tried workers' strikes, with little success. Subsequently, they resorted to a national boycott of the sale and consumption of table grapes. A key component of their strategy was to bring churches into their struggle and convince them to join the boycott.

This was a protest movement on a national scale, and the United Presbyterian Church in the United States of America was swept into it in a big way. For a number of years, the General Assembly voted to support their effort and called on all member churches to also support the boycott. This issue left us in San Joaquin Valley, the major source of grapes and raisins, increasingly in a quandary. Many in our local church were grape growers and were very distressed at this turn of events. They wondered how their mother denomination could be so insensitive to their situation. In effect, they were being asked to boycott their own produce.

These farmers were mostly small growers. They were at the mercy of the big corporation growers and packers who set the price of grapes and the workers' wages, against whom Cesar Chavez was struggling. Corporations housed the workers in living conditions that were decried as very poor and determined their wage scale and conditions in the fields. The small farmers had no choice but to go along with these big corporations and oppose the workers' union, for the sake of their own survival.

At that time I was the chair of the Social Concerns committee of our Presbytery of San Joaquin. After consulting with our synod executive, we organized for action. Ron Karabian, an elder from our church, was elected to be a commissioner to the next General Assembly, to take place in May of 1976 in Baltimore, Maryland. He was given an orientation on how the General Assembly committee system worked, where overtures for approval by the plenary session originated. His task was to get on the right committee and see what he could do to prevent the Assembly from adopting another pro-boycott resolution. This he was able to do. He succeeded in having an alternate resolution adopted which, in effect, was the first ever undertaken to study the plight of the small grape growers and understand the difficult position they were forced into by the boycott. After Ron came home, we all were jubilant and waited to see what would happen as a consequence.

To implement this resolution, the General Assembly approved the formation of a commission to study this issue and recommend action in regard to their report. First, I got a phone call from the executive of the national Social Action division of the United Presbyterian Church with a question, "Kass, what is going on there?"

"Well," I said, "how is it that you know me?"

"Oh, you are well known here!" he answered, to my surprise.

"We've appointed a task force to come there and see things from close-up."

"Who is on the task force?" I asked. "Is any member from our area on it?"

"They are from the San Francisco area, and their chairman is the Rev. John Turpin, pastor of First Presbyterian Church of Oakland," he replied.

"Then things are stacked up against us, because we have no representation on the task force," I observed with disappointment.

Several days later, it came to my attention that this task force was coming to Delano to interview Caesar Chavez in person. I immediately called a number of our presbytery committee members and said, "Get ready we are going to Delano." In answer to their puzzled inquiry as to why, I said, "This task force is coming into our presbytery's jurisdiction without notifying us first, which is not in proper Presbyterian order. We'll go and meet with them and see what they are up to."

So it was that we went to their motel room, knocked on the door, and introduced ourselves to a surprised and apprehensive group gathered for the occasion. After apologizing for their oversight, they agreed to have us accompany them when they went to interview Cesar Chavez. We all went together to the house where he and his leaders were staying. He was bedridden because of chronic back pain. We stood at his bedside and shared words of thanks for receiving us, and we explained why we needed his perspective on the question of the boycott. It was a short meeting, with not much substance except our thrill at being by his side for the occasion.

After this we went to a restaurant where we had a frank sharing of minds and hearts. At one point I asked a question, "Do you know what the small farmers in this area are going through and the dilemma in which our denomination's stance has placed us all?"

Their chair, John Turpin, said, "The suffering you are going through is that of taking up your crosses in obedience to Jesus Christ."

"In other words," I replied, "what you are expecting us to do is to take up our crosses and die! But how about you? What is the suffering you are willing to share? You are really saying that we should be willing to 'go to hell for the glory of God.' We are willing to do so, but we are inviting you all to join us on that journey!"

Before tempers got out of hand, we shared some more niceties and pleasantries and then bade our farewells. The upshot of it all was that the General Assembly, during the next year's session, adopted a paper for the study of the small farmers' problems and never again declared support of a total boycott of grapes and raisins.

Back in our presbytery, there was great satisfaction over developments at the General Assembly over the issue of the Grape Boycott. However, there was work for us to do still, because the issue of the plight of farm workers remained. After struggling with this question, we agreed to establish a community center for them where they could gather and their needs could be addressed. In Sanger, the United Methodist Church had a church facility that was closed. We negotiated with them for its use for this purpose, and our presbytery financed the hiring of a director to oversee its services.

Blessed Memories

Among the many loving memories we have of Fresno are those of my parents, who went to be with the Lord there. My mother, who suffered a variety of illnesses for years, the most serious of which was rheumatoid arthritis, died on September 19, 1971. My father died of a heart attack on December 17, 1974. They had served hard and long, loved family and community, and left an indelible witness to Jesus Christ as the source of their faith and their amazing years among us. They are buried in the Massis section of Ararat Cemetery in Fresno.

My brother Sarkis, who was six years my senior, died in 2000 in Greenville, Michigan. He was a most unusual, creative, and visionary man. I mentioned earlier that he ran away and joined the British Navy during World War II. Well, that spirit of adventure and risk taking was the hallmark of his personality. He came to America on a shoe string, and survived one way or another, until he met and married Olivette Trevanion, an amazing woman in herself. They eventually settled in the Grand Rapids, Michigan area and raised a family of four sons: Haig, Armen, Van, and Dicran. He bought a wreck of a house in Greenville, with a number of acres of timber and farming land. It was always his dream to have a farm, and this was it. However, when I saw the house I said, "You are going to live here?"

"Wait till you see how I'll rebuild it," he replied.

Well, he not only rebuilt it but expanded it to become Kassouni Farm. He was an industrialist who went into the plastics business and prospered in it. He was deep into Armenian nationalism, but in his own way. For several years he would get up, go to his favorite restaurant and settle in for an hour or two to write. His book was eventually published in 1996. Its title was How Armenia Can Be Free (Private publishing). He wrote in the days of the Soviet Union, which eventually fell apart in 1991. However, he knew how vulnerable the young republic would be among many adversaries. It was his dream that Armenia would offer its territory to the United Nations, provide troops for its world-wide operations, and thereby be free from subjugation by foreign powers, while gaining prominence in the family of nations. How about that?

He was visiting in our home on a Tuesday, ironically after a visit with Archbishop Barsamian, Eastern Diocese of the Armenian Church, who was very interested in his book. That's the last time we saw him. He went back home to Greenville, and two days later, on June 1, 2000, he died of a massive heart attack. All of Greenville grieved his loss because he was much loved and admired. We continued to gather at the Farm many times after that, and it became the venue for family gatherings for years following. As per his instructions, his ashes were spread in three countries: The forest behind their house, Lake Sevan in Armenia, and Larnaca, Cyprus.

Two of his sons, Haig, along with his wife Ann as Director of Human Resources, and Armen (Kim), continued the business and expanded it to be N-K Manufacturing Technologies LLC, in Grand Rapids, Michigan. Their third son Van (Luba), developed his own manufacturing business called Kassouni Manufacturing Inc., dealing with his own patented inventions. The fourth son, Dicran, moved back to Greenville from Alaska where he had moved to many years ago, and took over the Kassouni Farm. Thus, the legacy of his parents will be sustained into the next generation.

My First Pastorates

1. My first pastorate, Armenian Evangelical Church of New York City. Photo courtesy of AECNYC.
2. My second pastorate, First Armenian Presbyterian Church (FAPC), Fresno, California.
3. Convention of the Armenian Evangelical Union of North America at FAPC. *Front row, second from the left,* me.
4. Groundbreaking for the new Christian Education building, 1971.
5. We start building. Three generations of Kassounis.

Ministry in Fresno

1. Father and son build for the future.
2. The new sanctuary building, FAPC, 1975.
3. Dedication Service of the new sanctuary, June 13, 1976.
4. Clergy in attendance at the Dedication Service: Rev. Paul Avazian, Rev. Harry Missirlian, Rev. Bill Antablin, Rabbi David Greenberg.
5. The Statue of David of Sassoon, Varaz Samuelian, Fresno Courthouse Park.

Six

Our Move Out of Fresno

In the summer of 1977, I received a letter of inquiry from the chair of the pastor-seeking committee of the United Armenian Congregational Church of Los Angeles wanting to know if I'd be interested in the position of pastor. Their pastor, and my good friend, the Rev. Paul Avazian had died from cancer some time before, and they were in the search. Ultimately I was offered the position. After consulting with my wife and family, I accepted their call and made the big move to a new ministry that fall.

I had served FAPC for thirteen years, bringing it from the verge of collapse to membership close to three hundred, with a vibrant Sunday school and youth programs. Two of the three phases of the new building program were complete. God had blessed us mightily through all our trials, challenges, and struggles. It was time to move on and hand the reins to another pastor.

The pastor who followed me at FAPC was the Rev. Bernard Geukguezian. He and his wife, Knar, were good friends whom I had known for years. Interestingly, he followed me as a student at New York Biblical Seminary, then as youth director at the Armenian Presbyterian

Church of West New York, New Jersey. He was called to this church as pastor years later, and he served them with distinction. He was called to the pulpit of FAPC after my departure. I cherished our friendship immensely, especially so in my dark years.

Standing with me in full and loving support through all those years were my wife, Addie, and children, Linda, Nancy, Karen, and Timothy. Addie kept up her profession as a nurse and provided great financial, physical, moral, and spiritual support. However, our marital relationship had begun to show strains, yet her devotion was unswerving.

Let Me Brag A Little

Our three girls attended Roosevelt High School in Fresno and graduated before we moved. Tim attended Kennedy High School in Granada Hills, California.

Linda Joy attended California State University, Fresno, majoring in microbiology, with an eye on becoming a medical laboratory technician. She later earned her master's degree in that field from California State University, Long Beach, California. She remained single for a number of years until the right man came along. He is Steve Walker. They got married in 2001 and reside in Gold River, California. She has worked in several medical institutions and laboratories in Sacramento, mostly at Dignity Health, directing their medical labs. Steve works in Sacramento with a company that majors in demographic-related services. His real love and expertise is music, however. He has a recording studio and provides sound amplification and recording services to area concerts. He met Linda when he was recording a choral group called RSVP (Reconciliation Singers Voices of Peace) in which she was one of the singers.

Nancy Jean chose to go to Whitworth College in Spokane, Washington, a Presbyterian school. Her major was in business with an eye on hospital administration. She later went to Northwestern University in Evanston, Illinois, and earned her master's degree in hospital administration.

While there she fell in love and married Greg McGinnis of Jerry City, Ohio. He has his own company providing sales services for a number of building-related products. Nancy worked for many years in the Kaiser Permanente medical organization as an administrator. They have two sons, Paul and Gage, and a daughter Lauren.

Karen Martha attended Occidental College, in Eagle Rock (Los Angeles) California. Her major was in voice, with the goal of becoming an opera singer. While in college she fell in love and married Pete May of Arcadia, California. She continued her training in voice and sang in several operas in Northern California, where they had moved following her husband's medical school education and the beginning of his practice in dermatology in Napa, California. She has been the director of several girls' choirs in Napa High School, who have won several statewide awards in choir competitions. They have two sons, Spencer and Lucas, and a daughter Aubrey. On January 1, 2001, I had the joy and privilege of baptizing the boys at First Presbyterian Church, Napa, California.

Timothy Vartkes went on from Kennedy High School, Granada Hills, California, to the University of California at San Diego for two years, and he then transferred to the University of California at Berkeley. He majored in Philosophy, and from there he went on to Loyola Law School in Los Angeles. He passed the bar exams at first try and has been practicing law in Sacramento, California. He and his wife Amy started their own law firm called Kassouni Law, and their offices are close to the State Capitol, specializing in land use and property rights. Amy (Chaffin) comes from Hawaii where her dad was the chief executive of Kaiser Permanente, until his retirement several years go. They have two children, their son Alexander, and daughter Frances. I had the joy and privilege of baptizing Alexander on April 9, 2000, at Geneva Presbyterian Church in Laguna Hills, California, and his sister Frances on August 19, 2007, at Morningside Presbyterian Church in Fullerton, California.

There are many episodes in the life of these four children that stand out in my mind. They were all great kids and from childhood on demonstrated character and personality traits of being strong, intelligent, and ambitious people. Let me share several with my readers.

Linda always had music in her veins and pursued singing and acting as her avocation. She sang in a number of college musicals, and she also was very active in the Fresno Community Theater productions. One very early morning, past midnight, I received a telephone call from her saying, "Dad, I need you! I've been in a car accident. Could you come please?"

Well, she had gone to a cast party after one of their productions and was coming home late when she dozed and crashed the car, our special 1966 Ford Mustang. Luckily, she was alone and did not hit any buildings or people, but the car had jumped the curb, hit a sign post, and stopped short of a garage in an empty lot. Not only was she my precious daughter, but the car she was driving was my treasured 1966 Mustang! All's well that ends well. She was safe, and the car could be repaired.

Nancy pursued her dreams starting with her college education at Whitworth College, Spokane, Washington. She loved it there so much that two of her children have gone there since then. The episode I have relates to the day of her graduation, May 18, 1980. Addie and I had driven there with the intention of bringing her and her stuff back with us. We were at a Kmart store to buy a luggage rack for her belongings, when a woman approached us in the parking lot and said to me, "Mister, you'd better roll up your windows because a volcano has erupted, and ashes are headed our way!"

I thought she was a little "off" because the skies were blue and the sun was shining. But on the western horizon, there were dark clouds building up, and I thought a rainstorm was probably coming. We went into the school gym where the ceremonies were to be held. Sure enough, the announcement was made that Mount Saint Helens, 285 miles to the west of us, had erupted and ashes were headed in our direction. It did not take long for the skies to darken. Ashes with the consistency of talcum powder began to come down like snow. I stepped out of the gym and noticed darkness had descended, and the street lights had come on. One little black kid standing nearby reached out to me and said with fear in his voice, "Mister, are we all going to die?"

"No son, we're not going to die. Don't be afraid," I said, not knowing what was in store for us. Well, we were stuck there for three days not being able to drive anywhere because the streets and countryside were covered with several inches of volcanic ash. Driving through that would surely ruin a car's engine. We and a number of other parents were confined to student quarters during this event, and we began to show signs of being "stir crazy." The school administration came up with a very good idea to help us out, by asking Dr. Dale Bruner, a very popular professor, to lead us in a series of Bible studies. This he did, with a touch of tension-easing humor, on the topic "The Bible and the End of the World." When we finally left town, we first drove east to Idaho and then south to Nevada, and then home to California, bypassing Interstate 5 altogether.

On the way I said to Nancy, "You know why this happened on the day of your graduation? It's because when you were little I used to call you 'my little spitfire!'" I called her that because she had sparkling black eyes full of life and fun. They and family now reside in Elk Grove, California.

Karen, the youngest of the three, had a strong will. She never hesitated in doing what she'd set her mind on doing and being. As the third daughter, she had to put up with her sisters' games and jokes at her expense, such as their teasing by telling her she was adopted. (We did not know her sisters had said this till years later.) Both her sisters had participated in the Junior Miss Pageants and had won the Miss Fresno competition while in high school. When asked why she did not also go for that achievement, Karen said, "Because I don't want to follow my sisters." Well, God bless her, she soon proceeded to go on stage as an aspiring professional, and we heard her sing in a number of operas.

Our fourth is Timothy. Being the only son surrounded by three sisters, I feared that he would be overpowered by them. Actually, the opposite was true. We used to play a game where he used to chase them all over the house. They would run around and then come to hide behind, seated on our couch, in mock terror, seeking protection from him behind my back. The outstanding trait that emerged early in Tim was that of courage. He was not afraid to confront those who tried to take advantage of him. I realized that one day when he came home from elementary school. He told us that a bigger boy had taken his dime, which we gave him daily so he could buy his cup of ice-cream.

"So what did you do about it?" I asked.

"I took it back!" was his curt answer. I did not need to question him any further as to how he did it.

One day when he was in Junior High School I got a call from the principal. "Come to my office. Your son Tim is in trouble. He was in a fight with another student."

I hurried over and talked with Tim about this incident. It seems a bully had been swaggering around daring any to stand up to him. Well, evidently Tim did!

"Somebody had to stand up to him, Dad. I challenged him to a fight. We agreed to meet after school, and the word got out. The principal got wind of it and called me in. So now I am suspended from school for one day."

I asked the principal what measures they had in place to discourage bullies. He said they had no such measures.

"Well," I said, "it seems Tim has his way of doing it. Punishing him for this is rather hasty, don't you think? I'll talk to him and help him work through his feelings, so he'll be able to control himself in the future." With that we came to an amicable conclusion, and Tim could return to class again.

From Fresno, we made the move to Los Angeles in stages. In the fall of 1977, I came down to Los Angeles while the family stayed behind for a year, and I started my ministry at UACC. I rented a small apartment and started looking for a house, eventually deciding to buy a newly constructed one in Granada Hills with five bedrooms. Linda moved down to be with me in the new house before the others came. She did so to attend California State University at Long Beach to earn her Master's degree in microbiology.

A rude awakening one night introduced us to the realities of life in Southern California: screaming sirens of firetrucks racing to extinguish a range fire on the hills behind our house! We were fortunate that it was put out before it reached our street. Granada Hills is located just along the San Andreas Fault. We moved in after the devastating Sylmar Earthquake of 1971, which toppled bridges and broke up the highways in the vicinity. And we all had already moved out by 1994 when the big Northridge Earthquake struck. Whew!

My Third Pastorate, in Los Angeles

The contrasts between Los Angeles and Fresno were enormous. I was no longer in a small city with all members within a short distance of the church. UACC was three times the size of FAPC, and parishioners were spread out over many miles throughout metropolitan Los Angeles. My resolve to visit all members in their homes was put to an early and continuing test, as I had to drive long distances to call on them. The issue facing the church centered in the fact that Armenians in increasing number were immigrating to the area from the Middle East, and before too long from Armenia as well.

For example, the discussion at the first meeting of our Church Council was about a gift of $3,000, offered by a donor for the express purpose of putting the name of the church in Armenian characters below the one we already had in English. After lengthy debate (which was an eye-opener for me) the offer was refused, because the "Americanized Armenians" stressed that we were now all in America, and English would have to be the only language used for signage.

This issue of English or Armenian was also critical to the language used in our worship services. One group wanted to eliminate Armenian altogether, and at best they tolerated a five-minute sermon in that language. The other faction complained that we did not have enough Armenian and that it was offensive to them not to have their mother tongue as the primary language used in church services. So, I walked a fine line seeking to satisfy both camps. Since my "pulpit Armenian" was iffy, we secured the services of the Rev. Edward Tovmassian to preach a "short" Armenian sermon (leaving it up to him to decide the exact length). Then in 1981 we called the Rev. Berdj Djambazian from Lebanon to carry on that ministry, as our associate pastor.

This matter of which language to use was an issue in just about all programs of the church, such as the youth program. For example, one day a delegation of youth of recent immigrants came to me and said, "Pastor, there is prejudice against us in this church."

"What do you mean, and how is that?" I asked in response.

"They call us FOBs," they said, meaning Fresh Off the Boat.

With an instant flash of insight I replied, "Well, you call them SOBs!"

"How can we do that? It's not nice" they replied.

"No, it does not mean what you think. It stands for Stale Off the Boat," I said. Very soon after that a truce on name calling took place between the FOBs and the SOBs in our church.

Our struggle to grow a church with a clear mission to both "Americanized Armenians" who spoke little or no Armenian and also to new immigrants who spoke little or no English was a herculean task. Added to this was a third element, composed of representatives of both groups, who had a deep conviction that we should establish a school for the teaching of our language and heritage along with the Gospel. Heading this effort was Alice Haig, one of our members and a leader of long standing. She and I set out to determine the feasibility of such a venture. Standing ready to help out in this regard was the Armenian Missionary Association of America. The Rev. Dr. Giragos Chopourian, executive director of the AMAA, vigorously followed through to secure funding from Elise Merdinian, a member of our church, who had committed to leave her legacy to the AMAA for this very purpose.

A New School is Born

After several meetings of interested people and polling the feelings of the community on this cause, Alice Haig and I, supported by a small group of committed people, decided to go ahead and organize a school. It was to be totally independent of our church in terms of funding, organization, and administration. In 1982 it began operation with thirteen students, four staff people, and the Rev. Daniel Albarian, administrator and chaplain. After initial opposition to the request that classrooms in our church be allowed to be used to house it only for a few months, the church council granted permission. From there the C.(Charlotte) & E.(Elise) Merdinian Armenian Evangelical School moved to the Christian Education building of the North Hollywood Presbyterian Church, and from there to their present quarters in Sherman Oaks. It has grown to be a school of close to two hundred students, from elementary to ninth grades. It is a highly regarded institution, and, to date, the only school of its kind in the Armenian Evangelical communities of America.

John Mokkosian Joins Our Staff

In April of 1978, we had John Mokkosian join our staff as our assistant for Christian Education. He and his wife, Linda, and son, Luke, came to us from Philadelphia, Pennsylvania. His education for ministry was at Princeton Seminary (MDiv), and he had also studied at Haigazian College, and the Near East School of Theology in Beirut. He worked mostly with our youth and contributed meaningful support not only to me as pastor but the whole congregation. He was not yet ordained when he came to us, but since he had all the necessary education, we proceeded to his ordination in our church sanctuary on December 10, 1978, under the auspices of the Armenian Evangelical Union. Soon after, in February 1981, John received a call to the pastorate of Armenian Congregational Church, Salem, New Hampshire. I appreciated John's contributions very much indeed. It was a pleasure to have a staff leader who was not taken over by the glitz and overpowering version of evangelical Southern California theology. We had much in common and often shared our thoughts and feelings in support of each other.

Censorship Anyone?

While John was still with us, he and Ron Tovmassian, our youth leader, led a week-long youth retreat at the Presbyterian Conference Center at Big Bear Lake. Something happened there that illustrates the point I made in the previous paragraph. One evening during that week, we were having our board of deacons meeting with Dr. Sarkis Kalfayan, chairman. Almost at the end of our meeting, which always seemed to go to at least 11:00 p.m., a deacon (whose name I will withhold) spoke up. "Something has taken place during our youth retreat that is sheer blasphemy!"

Thus, he introduced an item that was not on the agenda. I had no clue what he was talking about and said so after everyone's eyes turned on me for a response. This deacon proceeded to say that a movie was shown to our youth that insulted our high regard for Jesus. When he mentioned the movie titled *Parable*. I immediately understood what he was talking about.

"Have you seen that movie?" I inquired.

"No, I have not, but I have a thick file about it" was his amazing response.

"Well," I said, "I've seen it, and I think it is a great film for our youth to see." With the tension rising significantly in the room, our chairman then asked me to let them know what the controversy was all about.

Parable was a movie planned and funded by the Protestant Council of the City of New York, for the express purpose of making it their one and only exhibit at the World's Fair in 1964, held on the same grounds of the 1939 World's Fair in Flushing, Long Island, New York. Interestingly, we were still living in Flushing then, only a mile away from the Fair. We all made it a point to go before we loaded up our station wagon and headed west to California. *Parable* was a very unusual film for a variety of reasons, which created controversy. This controversy was the deacon's source of the information he had gathered. The film was a totally silent one, by design, leaving it up to the viewer to watch and respond emotionally and intellectually.

The plot of this movie centered around a circus coming into town, very much like the Barnum and Bailey circuses used to do. Following the slow and deliberate march of circus wagons, show-people, elephants, and caged lions and bears, last of all came a donkey ridden by a man dressed in a clown's attire and makeup. The scene shifted to the circus itself, now settled in with the shows in progress. This lone "clown" was seen taking water to the thirsty animals, going stall to stall where they were kept, waiting for their turn to be taken to the circus floor for their acts.

A man sitting high and above all others near the ceiling created the focus of the acts. He manipulated a series of chords connected to a young woman on the floor below, all intentionally made to look very much like a puppet show. As this dark and menacing-looking man pulled the chords jerking his victim this way and that, up and down, the audience laughed and cheered. However, when the clown in our story saw this spectacle, he grew very disturbed. Unexpectedly, he took a knife in his hand, stepped into the spotlight, went to this poor girl, and cut the chords to set her free from the torture to which she was being subjected. This bold act of kindness on his part triggered the fury of the manipulator. Soon after that the clown was killed and disposed of for being so obstructive and an obvious impediment to the popularity of the show, which continued as before without his interventions.

The film then shifts to the circus leaving town. Just like the early scene, we have the wagons and the animals. But wait! At the very end is this clown, who had been murdered by the angry puppeteer, once again bringing up the rear very much like he did before. Thus the film ended, leaving it up to the viewers to ponder, discuss, and respond. The controversy centered not on the plot but the fact that obviously the person of Jesus was portrayed in the clown, his deeds, his death, and his resurrection.

"They turned Jesus into a clown!" was the cry of the traditionalists. This depiction of Jesus (as was the common interpretation) was considered to be an insult and a blasphemy. Hence our deacon's claim in his outburst.

Why have I told this story at length? Because it is a classic example, in terms of what I have encountered in my ministries, concerning intransigence and rush to judgment in matters of faith in and devotion to Jesus Christ as our Lord and Savior. However, the issue went far beyond that of viewing this film. It brought up the serious question of censorship.

"What should we do about this matter?" our chairman asked, turning to me for a solution.

"This is a very serious matter," I replied. "Are you now setting a new policy that films should be previewed by a special censorship committee, apart from the pastor, before it is seen by our youth?" I knew all about this film, and when John Mokkosian, their leader, asked me if it was an appropriate film for their use, I was fully supportive.

The upshot of it was that, thankfully, they left it up to me with a cautionary note that we should be careful in the future in such matters.

The most unusual part of this story is yet to come. That very same month, the Rev. Dr. Don Buteyn, associate pastor of the world-famous Hollywood Presbyterian Church (Dr. Lloyd Ogilvie, senior pastor), was invited by our board of deacons and Christian Education board to lead us in a "Spiritual Emphasis and Renewal" series of talks during a weekend. He was our preacher for the Sunday service. In the course of his sermon, he challenged us to follow in the spirit of Jesus and reach out with love to marginalized people in society. To illustrate his theme, he recounted the story of this very same film, *Parable*, and commented what a great thing it would be if we all could view it as well. Dr. Kalfayan, the chairman of our deacons, told me afterward what a great sermon it was, and that maybe we could have our couples group view it sometime!

"Do you know that he was speaking of the same film we were all so shook up about in our deacons' meeting recently?" I asked. He was amazed at this fact and immediately realized how we can get carried away, prematurely condemn people, and judge them unfairly. I'm grateful I was able to defend my colleague and take the heat to avoid a situation that could have been devastating.

So much for the act of "blasphemy" which was supposedly committed at our youth retreat. This incident often reminds me of how we can, and sometimes do, actually abuse people in the name of true faith. And in doing so we inflict harm on the body of Christ, the church.

The other youth leader who was with John for this youth retreat was Ron Tovmassian, son of our former associate pastor, the Rev. Edward and Arous Tovmassian. He was a seminarian at Fuller Seminary. While still with us at UACC, he received a call to his first pastorate, the Armenian Memorial Church in Watertown, Massachusetts. Before he and his wife, Renee, went there, Ron was ordained to the Christian ministry in our sanctuary on August 28, 1983. Thus we had two ordinations during my time at this church.

Berdj Djambazian, Our Associate Pastor

The pressing need for pastoral support for us in the area of Armenian language became increasingly clear as immigrants continued to come in growing numbers. After a search for the right person, a call was extended to the Rev. Berdj Djambazian to be the associate pastor of United Armenian Congregational Church of Los Angeles. At that time he was residing in France, so we sponsored his immigration. He and family including his wife Shoghig, son Danny, and daughters Helene and Pauline came to California in September 1981. He was an evangelist and pastor who had served the Nor Marash church in Beirut and in Germany and France. He was fluent in six languages: Armenian, Turkish, Arabic, English, French, and German. He and his brother Hagop (James) had worked extensively together as a team carrying on evangelistic missions in the Middle East and in Europe. Hagop was a composer and musician, contributing extensively in the area of music and songs in the traditional Armenian genre. He directed outreach to Armenians via Trans World Radio, carrying the message of Christ to our people all over the world. Berdj was ministering in France when he received our call.

I had met him several years before, and we had "clicked" in terms of our faith and our understanding of the issues that faced us in America. "We need you in America, Berdj," I said to him. "As Jesus said, 'the fields are ripe for harvesting.' This is like the Macedonian call that Paul received to take the Gospel into Europe, 'Come over and help us.'" So it was that he heard the call and finally agreed to come. He filled his niche in our church very well, in preaching, teaching, and ministering. He joined me in researching the need for a new church in East Hollywood. Several years later, after my departure Berdj assumed the position of pastor for twelve years, and then he was followed by the Rev. Dr. Peter Doghramji as senior pastor.

A New Church is Born

The influx of new immigrants from Soviet Armenia had escalated, with more and more being allowed to leave their country. In increasing numbers they were coming to settle in East Hollywood. That district was formally called "Little Armenia," and city maps designated it as such. It became obvious to me that since our church was out of their geographic area, they should have a church of their own. Enough leaders agreed with me, and with the help of the Armenian Evangelical Union and the Armenian Missionary Association, we went about organizing one. We called the Rev. Abrahan Jizmejian, from Canada, to come and be the evangelist for this mission, which he did until the time was right to call a full-time pastor.

In 1981 the new church became a reality with the call of the Rev. Abraham Chaparian as pastor. Armenian Evangelical Church began its ministries in a rented facility of the American Baptist Church. Eventually they bought a building on Franklin Avenue, with the aid of the AMAA. They have grown significantly, and now, thirty-four years later, they are growing and thriving.

Not only were the spiritual needs of these recent immigrants addressed but also their social needs as well, with the opening of the Armenian Evangelical Social Service Center on Santa Monica Blvd in 1979 (in East Hollywood). It was the vision of the Rev. Jirair Sogomian, pastor of Immanuel Armenian Congregational Church, Downey, and the strong support of Mr. James Koundakjian that got the project rolling in its infancy. Under the leadership of Mr. Hagop Loussararian, it grew significantly, necessitating their move to Glendale. There they purchased a building on Colorado Blvd. and served thousands of our immigrant people for many years. In 2012, growing services provided by governmental agencies made the continuation of the Social Service Center redundant. Consequently they ceased to function, the building was sold, and the proceeds donated to the C. & E. Armenian Evangelical School.

An Assassination Remembered

Our church held a prominent and highly visible position within the Armenian community throughout the greater Los Angeles area and the whole nation as well, being the largest church of its kind in the United States. As their pastor, I was always very aware of this fact, and there were times when that fact was put to the test.

One such event of critical import caught us all unprepared and called on us to take a public stand. On the morning of Thursday, January 28, 1982, at 9:28 a.m., Kemal Arikan, the Turkish consul general, was shot dead by a young Armenian radical by the name of Hampig Sassounian. He was a member of Justice Commandos Against Armenian Genocide. The shooting happened while Arikan was riding in a car in Beverly Hills going to his office. The news spread like wildfire, and we were all stunned. I knew that on Sunday morning, the congregation would be in a tizzy about this matter. Many people would be asking "Why?" and "What would we say about this?" In my own mind I pondered what to say to our congregation.

After thinking and praying hard about this issue, I opted not to make any announcement by way of news but to incorporate my thoughts in my pastoral prayer. Sunday morning, before the prayer, I announced that I was going to read my prayer to the congregation before I prayed it. Any who did not agree with the position I was taking on the matter of the crime committed on Thursday could leave the sanctuary or not say "Amen" following my prayer. After reading it, several people did leave the room. In summary, here is what I prayed:

"Gracious God, we are greatly troubled by the events that took place last Thursday. We are perplexed in our whole community as to what we could do or say. We are a people who have experienced your redeeming grace in Jesus Christ. Help us to act as those who reflect His presence among us. We first pray that your Spirit will bring comfort to the family of the slain diplomat, who was killed in revenge for the plight of our people during and following the Genocide. As survivors of the Genocide, we mourn the loss of our people dearly. While doing so we also reach out in love to his family who are now engulfed in grief. We also pray for Hampig Sassounian, a young man who has been overwhelmed by his desire for justice for our people. We pray that from out of the many conflicting and confusing voices now engulfing him, he will hear your clear voice of judgment and grace. May he understand and accept the implications of his action, and may your Spirit touch his heart and mind to find forgiveness and divine compassion. We are all sinners, who pray for and seek your redeeming touch in Christ our Lord, who died that we all may live."

Well! When the news got out that "Kassouni had prayed for the Turkish consul," who was slain in the cause of justice for our people, as the saying goes, "All hell broke loose!" I began to receive all kinds of phone calls, one even from the editor of the *Armenian Reporter*, in New York, asking me if it was true that I had said a mass for the slain consul.

My reply was, "No, I did not pray for him but for his family, and you know we don't say mass for the dead in our services. We are evangelicals."

Angry letters to editors of local papers were written, and one man even challenged me to a public debate, saying, "I throw my gauntlet before him and am ready to debate this matter!"

It was very encouraging when Hampig Sassounian's uncle came to me in person, and instead of angry words of recriminations, which I expected, he told me, "Hold yourself strong, and tell that man that Hampig's uncle picks up his gauntlet and will gladly debate him."

One night, unknown perpetrators slashed the tires of our people's cars who were attending a council meeting at the church. Following that I received a call from one of our members telling me that certain leaders of the community wanted to come and meet with me. Things were getting very serious! I knew that some people would at times resort to violence in the service of their cause, so I braced myself and feared for my physical safety.

Soon after, a group of three men plus a member from our church who had initially called me came to meet with me in my church office. I took the initiative, and after welcoming them, I said, "Allow me to say a few words. I want you to know who I am and whose son I am. I am a proud Armenian who has not hesitated to work in our cause in America in a variety of ways. I could enumerate them for you, if you so desire. Second, I am the son of Manuel Kassouni. He was a well-known and respected leader. His exploits in Aintab, on behalf of Armenian students, were legendary. I follow in his footsteps in advocating for our rights. Third, I want to inform you that I am the moderator of the Armenian Evangelical Union, comprised of over twenty-five churches throughout America. I have notified them of this impending crisis among us, and that if any harm were to come to me, they should be ready to respond in loud protest. Let us now proceed and discuss what brings you here today."

"Badveli, please, we intend no harm to you," one of them said. "However, we want to know why you spoke out as you did from your pulpit last Sunday. You are the only clergy in Los Angeles who did so. Why did you not keep your silence, like all the other clergy did?"

"I am sorry, but something of this importance to all of us cannot go with no comment from our religious leaders. Others may opt to say nothing. I am different," I replied. We left it at that, and no violence against us came of it, for which I was very thankful. Today, Hampig is serving a life sentence in prison, and several requests for parole have been denied to him. I personally would support a move to have parole granted him for a variety of reasons.

The reason I spoke up the way I did was that the Armenian community in America had worked diligently over many years to develop an identity of hard-working, law-abiding citizens. It was an oft-repeated saying that one could find no Armenians in America's jails. To murder someone in the cause of our Genocide victims would tarnish the honor their memory has bestowed on us, and it would be replaced by the image of a violent and vindictive people.

Ministry in Los Angeles

United Armenian Congregational Church (UACC),
Los Angeles, California, 1978 - 1983.

UACC Executive Committee, 1982.
Front row, second from right, Dr. Sarkis Kalfayan, Chairman.

UACC Program Staff.

UACC Office Staff.

Our Children & their Families, from the 1990s to the Present

My children: *Left to right: seated,*
Karen Martha, Nancy Jean, Linda Joy;
standing, me, Timothy Vartkes.

My four children, ca. 2015. *Left to right:*
Timothy, Karen, Linda, and Nancy.

Linda and Steve Walker.

Dr. Pete and Karen May with their family.
Left to right: Pete, Aubrey Laura Kassouni, Lucas Owen, Karen, and Spencer Lewis.

Nancy and Greg McGinnis with their family.
Clockwise: Lauren Adrina, Paul Gregory, Gage William, Nancy, and Greg.

Timothy and Amy Kassouni with their family.
Left to right: Amy, Frances Evan, Alexander Timothy Kaleo, and Timothy.

Timothy and family, 2010.

My children with their cousins: Sarkis and Olivette Kassouni's sons Armen, Dicran, and Haig, and Nouvart's son Ted, ca. 2000. *Left to right, rear:* Armen, Linda, Dicran, Karen, Haig, Nancy, Tim, and Ted; *front:* Olivia and Jacob, Armen and Kim's children.

My Grandchildren!

Happy birthday time, ca. 1994.

A happy group, ca. 2003.

Seven

CRISIS IN MY MARRIAGE AND BEYOND

Among faults and failures that I had in my life, I confess that the failure of my marriage to Addie was the biggest one. Tensions and conflicts along the way in our marriage of twenty-nine years were signs that something big was brewing. It finally happened, like the eruption of a volcano, toward the close of 1983. Events in my personal life intervened and drove a wedge between us. I knew that I could not continue at UACC as its pastor. Before the church became aware of what had happened, I resigned. My last Sunday in the pulpit there was on February 12, 1984.

The moderator of the church council, Dr. Sarkis Kalfayan, was aware of the circumstances and at my request did not reveal them to the council until I had departed. In an article printed in the *Herald* (monthly newsletter of the church), he wrote about my departure and with gracious words paid a compliment to my six years as pastor:

> We at UACC are grateful for his devoted ministry here, as well as for the service he rendered to the Armenian Community in Southern California. He was instrumental in establishing the "Hollywood Outreach" program which now includes the Armenian Evangelical Social Service Center (founded by the

late James Koundakjian and Rev. Jirair Sogomian), the new Hollywood Church and other social and religious ministries. He showed sensitivity to the needs of fellow Armenians who have been immigrating to Southern California from foreign lands, during the past several years, and urged this Church to address their needs with understanding and charity…Reverend Kassouni showed notable leadership qualities in his role as administrative head-of-staff of the Church as well as the spiritual head of his flock. He was innovative in his ministry and was well organized. He will be long-remembered for his qualities of gentleness, constructive thinking and the rare ability to function effectively under duress.

After my departure, UACC extended a call to the Rev. Berdj Djambazian to take the position of senior pastor. This he did for several years, and following him the position was extended to the Rev. Dr. Peter Doghramji.

The breakup of our marriage did not follow immediately after I left UACC. For several months I continued to live at home, and Addie was most gracious in going along and accepting me in that regard. Since I resigned from my position in UACC, I was not sure in which direction I should go from there. Knowing also that no Armenian church would want my services, I went to see the executive presbyter of San Fernando Presbytery, who knew me personally. Without any hesitation she offered me the position of interim pastor of First Presbyterian Church of Palmdale, whose pastor had quit without notice, and they were in dire need. I accepted gratefully and commuted from our home in Granada Hills six days a week to Palmdale.

Out of the Armenian Church Community

For the first time in my life, I started a ministry in a non-Armenian church. I had often thought that this would be the direction my ministry would eventually take, but not under such circumstances. The church in Palmdale was in sad condition, and there was talk that it would probably have to close. However, Palmdale was in a building boom, and with new buildings going up all around in that part of town, I told the church leaders, "One would have to work hard to close this church. You are in a natural growth neighborhood. Let's go to work and grow again."

My priority in doing that was to visit every home of our church members and to start a youth group, since they'd not had one for quite some time. We succeeded in doing so, and hope was rekindled that they had a future. The turnaround was established with the coming of their next pastor, the Rev. Jim Barstow, who not only brought in new people but had a school built on the premises, with scores of children enrolled.

While I was still in Palmdale, I sent out feelers for where I could serve next, knowing I would need another assignment after eight months. I knew Dr. John Chandler, the executive presbyter of Los Ranchos Presbytery (Orange County) and went to talk with him in Anaheim, California. When he heard my story, he said, "Kass, I've known you for many years. I know the good work you did in Fresno, and we need you in this presbytery. Tustin Presbyterian Church is searching for an interim pastor. I will recommend you to be considered for that position." The search committee interviewed me and extended to me a call to their church, which I accepted. So my focus shifted to Orange County, and I began a new ministry there in the fall of 1984.

Tustin Presbyterian Church's beloved pastor, the Rev. Dr. Howard Jamieson, had retired after fourteen years of service, leaving a strong church of almost nine hundred members with a great history. It was 101 years old that year. They had just celebrated their centennial before I arrived there.

I commuted from our home in Granada Hills Saturday evening through Thursday morning, and I rented a room in the home of Betty Miller, at the corner of Heathcliff and La Loma, as a place to stay while in town. She was a highly regarded elder in the church, who made her home available as a matter of service. She had plenty of room in her house because her three children were all grown up and living elsewhere.

It was an arrangement that worked fine for me for several months, and it became my new home, even after I left Tustin Presbyterian Church in January of 1987.

Our marriage situation did not improve during those months even though we went for marriage counseling, and we finally separated. As a consequence, my move to Tustin became semipermanent. I met with each one of our children and spoke to them candidly about what had happened. I assured them of my deep love for each one, and that I would do all I could to support them in the future. The only one still at home with Addie was our son Tim, who was in transition between college (Berkeley) and law school (Loyola). Karen was married to Pete May, Nancy was married and living in Arcadia, and Linda was also married and living in Las Vegas. After shedding many tears and talking things out, we accepted the turn of events. We all picked up the broken pieces, as best we could, and with God's help began the hard task of reshaping our lives. Addie stayed in the house with Tim who went on to college soon after. She eventually sold the house and moved to Elk Grove, California, near her daughter, Nancy, and family, where she resides to this day.

A Turning Point

My ministry as head-of-staff of Tustin Presbyterian Church began in November 1984. It was a turning point for me in a number of ways. I was received with open arms, allowing me to lead them with no reservations. We had two services every Sunday morning, with Christian Education classes in between called "Bridgeway." Our associate pastor, Rev. Rex McDaniel, who had continued in that capacity which began with the previous pastor, Dr. Howard Jamieson, provided great support. We had a very positive ministry there together, until he received a call to another pastorate near Baltimore and left us in June of 1985.

In December 1984, in the church's publication, called *Tustin Presbyterian Press*, I wrote a Christmas meditation that essentially stated my core mission there in parable form. It is titled, "Come Walk with Me to Bethlehem":

Come, walk with me to Bethlehem...

It is a pilgrim's call. No tour guide here, with promises and guaranteed comforts on a two-week "Holiday Adventure," designed for busy people who must see it all, and then return to friends and home.

Come, walk with me to Bethlehem...

"Pilgrims are a sorry lot. They seem far out of place and out of date, looking, searching, probing, seeking... 'Which way to Bethlehem, please?' What's wrong with New York and Los Angeles? With all our modern facilities, scientific discoveries, who needs Bethlehem anymore?"

Come, walk with me to Bethlehem...

"Pilgrims are dull people who don't understand reality. They don't have to go so far at all. Bethlehem has come to us, has it not? In the comfort of our couches we can turn TV on and see not only Bethlehem but a thousand other places, from little chapel to crystal cathedrals! Yes, pilgrims are a sorry lot. They insist on long, tiring trips, and senseless journeys. Why ever leave our USA?"

Come, walk with me to Bethlehem...

Far away from crowded stores and rushing hordes, from pleading preachers and plastic believers, let us go far, far away. Let us take that inward walk, deep into the heart of God. Let us stretch our minds far out to probe the boundaries of human thought.

Come, walk with me to Bethlehem...

We will pass by Jerusalems with lofty temples, where priests with motion perpetual tend to sacred ritual, ignoring needs of hurting people, and smoke of burning sacrifice frees neither soul nor touches God. Let us skirt the palaces where Herods live in worldly splendor, plotting all the while to kill innocents untold. Walk, walk right by and leave behind such senseless plays and tricks of man, until we come to Bethlehem!

Come, walk with me to Bethlehem...
> *Our journey will bring us to the blessed place at last. Somewhere,*
> *some distant point far down the road will mark the spot. The star*
> *that guides will lead us on until it stops where Christ is born.*

Come, walk with me to Bethlehem...
> *The light that shines will illumine minds to see the Child, to call him*
> *"Lord!" That scene sublime will hush the tongue; on bended knee we*
> *shall confess with reverence and awe, "It surely was worth it all; to*
> *lose the world but find our soul!"*

Come with me to Bethlehem.

Along with preaching of sermons, teaching of adult-level classes was my joy there. I have always said that the health of a church can be seen in its adult-level classes and groups, and that I would always want to teach in that regard. I had already tried that in Fresno with some success, but this was for me much more challenging. These were highly educated people with advanced academic degrees. The church was located in the heart of Tustin's historic Old Town. I offered a series of classes with topics relevant to our faith as Presbyterians. Some of these were, "Understanding the Bible: Its Development, Its Authority and Its Use," "Understanding the Book of Revelation," and "The Prophecy of Habakkuk and the Problem of Suffering." I have kept my notes from these, and all the other lectures I have given over the span of forty years have also been saved. These will probably form the contents of another book I intend to write.

Our worship services were something special, mostly because of the outstanding choral music, under the direction of Bob Volbrecht. He led a choir of forty members, and they sang like the proverbial angels. For example, one Sunday they were going to sing Vivaldi's Gloria. Bob and I cooperated in its preparation, and we agreed that that morning I would have no sermon, but there would be a pause at which time we would celebrate Holy Communion. That's it: Vivaldi at first, then communion, followed by Vivaldi again with a climactic finish. When that service was over I thought I had died and gone to heaven! I often told

Bob, "The choral ministry at TPC is the best kept secret in our whole presbytery."

A high priority of mine was that of visitation, to the hospitalized, the shut-ins, and the bereaved. This also included a regular calling on the members in their homes. To be able to learn their names and connect them with the many faces before me in church, I asked Jere Murphy to stand across the street from the entrance after several services and take photos of everyone coming out and shaking my hand. This was in the days before digital cameras. He would have the negatives developed, and then we would sit at a table and go over each one and write their names on the back of the prints.

Calling people by their names in church, and then asking if I could visit with them in their homes was for me a great way of getting to know them. I soon developed the reputation that "Pastor Kass visits everybody in the church," although that never really happened. I've had many precious times spent with the elderly members, often during and after their hospitalization.

Administration of the church's many programs, and seeing to it that all parts of the system functioned well was the responsibility of the session (board of elders) of which I was the moderator (as it is in all Presbyterian churches). This is the nerve center of the church, and for me an extremely important matter which I did not take lightly. My approach to this function was first to spend time with each elder, especially the chairs of the various committees, to prepare with them how we were to address issues that were brought to the whole body. No surprises, please! Then, early on we set a ground rule. The time frame was to be from 7:30 p.m. till 9:00 p.m. No long, tedious, and frustrating sessions would be tolerated. My policy was, "We end our meetings at nine o'clock. After that, if you want to stay longer, you're welcome to do so, but I will be gone."

Humor was a key and necessary ingredient of my strategy in leading the session as well as the congregation. Pastors with no sense of humor consign themselves to boring and frustrating ministries. Humor, carefully and wisely used, breaks up logjams and maintains a joyful relationship in meetings, whether formal or informal. As an example, I remember when in one meeting the matter of the annual membership survey mandated by our denomination came up. There was one question which puzzled them: "How many among your session members are of racial/ethnic origin?" They all looked at each other, and then turning to me said, "We guess it's only you, Kass."

I responded with humor. "I don't know about that. I am Armenian and Armenia is in the Caucasus Mountains, from where the term 'Caucasian' comes. So I myself am Caucasian, but I don't know about the rest of you!" Come to think of it, I'm not sure how that question was answered in the survey document.

Humor is different from telling jokes. Skilled use of appropriate jokes has its place in informal gatherings and in small groups. The pulpit is not the place for them. Pastors who are comedians in the pulpit degrade the sanctity of the pulpit and bring dishonor upon themselves.

After serving TPC for one year and four months, I received a call to Christ Presbyterian Church of Huntington Beach to be their stated supply pastor on a two-thirds time basis and to be the coordinator for Church Development of Los Ranchos Presbytery in Anaheim with the other third.

From Tustin to Huntington Beach

This move was far different from a routine change of parishes because for the first time I began serving not only as pastor but as a presbytery executive. This dual role was a big challenge and also an exciting one. Dr. John Chandler, presbytery executive, who had encouraged me to make the move to Tustin, asked me if I'd be interested in joining his staff at Los Ranchos Presbytery on a part-time basis. They were in the process of raising $10,000,000 for new church development and also for redevelopment of existing churches, and they needed someone to implement that program. It was a tall order indeed, but I accepted it with enthusiasm. It was a new direction, a new area of ministry for me, and I welcomed it.

In February 1986, I began serving Christ Presbyterian Church. Deep in my soul I was struggling with the implications of my marital crisis. Should I keep it a secret from the church or not? How should I broach the subject, because I did not want to serve under false pretenses. Consequently, with much fear and anxiety at the start of our first meeting, I told the session, "I need to share something with you that's very important. I am separated from my wife, and a divorce is in the offing. If this will be considered problematic by you, please let me know, and I would be glad not to begin my ministry here."

After total silence for a minute or two, one elder, who was a big man physically, got up and came to me with outstretched arms. He gave me a big hug, saying, "Brother, we are here for you to support you. We want you to stay and carry on your ministry, and we will be praying for you." He was joined by all the others. With that action of affirmation on their part, a big load was lifted off my heart and shoulders, freeing me up to begin a new chapter in my life and ministry.

For one whole year, this church became like a close family to me. They were a small congregation of fewer than three hundred members, but the size contributed to a climate of warmth and intimacy within which we worshipped, fellowshipped, and served together for one year. I took my belongings from our house and moved them to a storage room of the church, not knowing what the future held for me. Physically, I was in limbo, but spiritually I was ready to take on whatever God had for me.

Lona Fowler has a poem titled "Middle Time" which captures my state of mind at that time. Here is the first verse from it:

"Between the exhilaration of Beginning and the satisfaction of Concluding is the Middle time of enduring, changing, trying, despairing, continuing, becoming..."

I was indeed in my "Middle Time," looking back with much nostalgia to all that had transpired in my life that now seemed so distant from me. I looked forward with hope and faith, but I had no guarantees that all would work out. So, I took the plunge, or leap, of faith and pressed on.

That was the year I was divorced, bringing to an end our marriage of thirty-three years to Addie. My recollections gathered in this book cannot even begin to address what those years held for us. At best, we had a beautiful family, and we celebrated many good times together. In the eyes of the beholder, we had "the ideal family," as my daughter Nancy put it. However, it really was not that. I have alluded to tensions and problems we faced, much of it, I must confess, from inner turmoil that existed in me from the beginning. My spiritual and moral fall in that regard has been real, and I do not dismiss it as being trivial at all.

However, as real as my fall has been, so has God's grace, lifting me up and restoring to me "the joy of my salvation," as the Psalmist says. Many were the days and nights when the demons of despair and defeat almost consumed me. I considered myself no longer fit for ministry and began to think in terms of leaving pulpit and church. I was shunned by friends, and it was fifteen years before any Armenian colleague in ministry (with one exception) talked to me. God's loving kindness held me steady through it all. My children never hesitated to maintain the bonds of love for me. If it had been different, I would have died! New friends came alongside, and with their encouragement and support I was able to carry on. I remain deeply thankful and will continue to hold them gratefully in my heart always.

Interim Ministries

1. Tustin Presbyterian Church (TPC), 1984 – 1986.
2. TPC Sanctuary and Chancel Choir.
3. TPC Coffee time.
4. Conversing with two TPC "Pillars of the Church", now with the Lord. *Left to right:* George Trotter Jr., me, and Elmer Farnsworth.

1.   TPC celebration of my 80th birthday.
2.   Not only cake but Samira's baklava!
3.   TPC children sharing their Sunday School art work.
4.   Christ Presbyterian Church, Huntington Beach, 1987 – 1988.

Geneva Presbyterian Church (GPC),
Laguna Woods, 2001 - 2002.

Dedication of GPC's new chapel.

Family gathering in celebration of the baptism of two week old Alexander,
son of Timothy and Amy Kassouni, baptized by his grandfather
on April 9, 2000, at Geneva Presbyterian Church.

1. Yorba Linda Presbyterian Church (YLPC), 2003 – 2006.
2. Celebration cake, March 25, 2006.
3. Samira recognized for her services with a rose presented by Marlies Lunger.
4. Time for the children's message.
5. YLPC Youth Choir.

1. Morningside Presbyterian Church (MPC), Fullerton, 2007 – 2008. Celebrating the 50th Anniversary of my ordination.
2. Surrounded by MPC preschool children.
3. The baptism of Frances Evan Kassouni, August 19, 2008, at MPC.
4. First Presbyterian Church, Garden Grove, 1997 – 1999.

Eight

My Marriage with Samira Audeh

First Presbyterian Church of Santa Ana was the place where Samira Audeh and I were joined in marriage on December 20, 1987. It was a simple ceremony, with the Rev. Dr. John Chandler (the executive presbyter of Los Ranchos Presbytery) officiating. The Rev. Tim Hart-Andersen (my colleague and associate executive presbyter) was my best man, and Mona (Sami) Bawarshi (Samira's sister) was the matron of honor. Samira and I had met five years earlier in Los Angeles, and now we both began a new life facing our future together. She was the third daughter of the Rev. Dr. and Mrs. Farid Audeh of Beirut, Lebanon. Her other sister was Samia (Samir) Abu-Jawdeh, also of Beirut. Dr. Audeh was the renowned pastor of the Evangelical Congregational Church of Beirut. He was the head of the Protestant community in Lebanon and their representative in the Government.

Samira is a marvelous woman. She is warm in personality and of very high intelligence. People near and far have a very high regard for her friendship and devotion without partiality. Her devotion to me personally is exemplary. She has contributed greatly to the regaining of my self-worth. Her constant support respective to the demands and challenges of life has contributed extensively to our happiness together. I hope I have in turn done my share to support her in all her needs also.

Her academic credentials, with an MA in Education from Azusa Pacific University, qualified Samira to tackle the challenging demands of educating our youth. Having been a teacher for over twenty years, she was hired by Irvine Unified School District and quickly ascended the ladder to the position of teacher on special assignment (TOSA). Her specialty was English language development. Students from seventy-six different language groups have been pouring into the school district. Samira is now in charge of the government-mandated testing program that determines the English proficiency level of all incoming students. Many of them are from the Middle East, but most are from Asian countries. Consequently she is an interpreter as well, going far beyond classroom duties. She has also developed a program for parents who do not speak English. Key to this is cross-cultural communication and appreciation. It has grown to be very popular. Parents who have been reluctant to attend now do so heartily. During her first year they had five hundred students tested. In 2016 they had almost seven thousand. That's how much the program has grown in twenty-five years.

Samira has the gift of loving hospitality. Her talent as a cook of Lebanese foods is known and acknowledged by all who've had the good fortune of tasting her delicacies. Whether it's at home with one of our dinner parties, or at a church social, she contributes generously with love. She has added her presence and support in the many church-development related activities that I have led. Thus it is that we have formed a team not only at home in our life together but in the public arena as well.

Into Uncharted Waters

At the start of my ministry in New York, a layman and I were talking about the pros and cons of ministering exclusively among Armenians. He said, "In an Armenian church and community, you will be a big fish in a small pond. In a non-Armenian ministry you will be a small fish in a big pond. Which do you want?"

Well, I was now, by virtue of circumstances in my life, in the big pond of the Presbytery of Los Ranchos as an associate executive presbyter. I began full-time work there in 1988. LRP (Los Ranchos Presbytery) was located in Anaheim and served some fifty-five churches and missions, with close to thirty thousand members. My entry into that stream of ministry was at a time when South Orange County's growth was booming. Before our very eyes, thousands of acres of farmland (mostly citrus fruit) were being eliminated, and housing and shopping developments were replacing them. I used to quip that the name of our presbytery should be changed from Los Ranchos to Los Developmentos! To meet the challenge that such growth presented to the Church, our presbytery was in the process of raising funds in a program called MOOD (Mission on Our Doorstep). A master plan for new church planting had been drawn up, in accordance with a careful study of the area by Dr. Bob Worley, of McCormick Seminary in Chicago. They were now ready to make their move. That's when I was called on to be their staff resource person to help make it happen.

Eccesiastical Obstetrics

I prayed for wisdom and courage to go full speed ahead, and for unity in our staff relationships so that our team would work smoothly and effectively. Our executive presbyter, Dr. John Chandler, had much experience in church development, and he was the leader. Rev. Tim Hart-Andersen, another associate executive presbyter, was in charge of the fund-raising and public relations. He and I worked closely together.

Our first project was a new church development in the city of Laguna Niguel. Several acres in the center of the city had been already purchased for this purpose, with a plan to sell part of it to a commercial developer with a joint-use agreement for use of their parking lot by the church on Saturdays and Sundays. This approach made the project financially feasible, freeing up the money for other new church startups.

It all began with a big sign saying, "Future Site of a Presbyterian Church," which Tim Hart Andersen and I took to the location. We actually planted the sign in the ground of that empty lot together. Following that, it was my job to reach out into the community, identify those who would want to support such a project, and gather them for fellowship and worship once a month. We met for this purpose in the community center located in the Crown Valley Community Park. In this endeavor, my wife Samira joined me, contributing much-needed support, all the way from going door to door and distributing invitations to our gatherings, to providing food and delicious pastries for the social times. She became famous for her baklava (a pastry made of philo dough, walnuts, pistachios, and syrup and cut in little squares, or shaped in little rolls) and sesame cookies. We called this aspect of our program "Baklava Evangelism!"

New church development is not an exact science. Various factors go into a successful enterprise. First, is the commitment of resources by a parent entity, preceded by a vision for church growth. In our case it was the Presbytery of Los Ranchos which had, under the leader of Dr. John Chandler, secured the necessary startup funds in the drive called Mission On Our Doorstep, or MOOD. Second, the genius of the program was that many congregations and many individual people were involved in the effort. Without that critical factor, just the money would not have done it.

My position in this exciting enterprise was that of the initiating pastor. My job was to do the preliminary work of gathering an initial group of people, start having Bible studies and fellowship gatherings, until the time came for the calling of the organizing pastor. The pastor who was ultimately chosen was the Rev. Kenneth McCullen, to whom I handed over all the duties involved and moved on to my next assignment. My first project was thus concluded.

The day came when they built their beautiful new sanctuary in Laguna Niguel. There was a special service for its dedication, and the climactic moment was the placing of the cross on the top of the roof. Before it was raised, we all were invited to sign our names on it. I joined in that exciting event and signed my name in Armenian, thus providing a touch of variety. It was then raised up high by a crane and placed in its groove as we all sang, "Lift high the Cross, the love of Christ proclaim till all the world adore his sacred name." I've often wondered how indelible was the ink of the pen I used for the occasion, and whether it is still there to this day.

This scenario was repeated in three other communities: Rancho Santa Margarita (a new community several miles east of Mission Viejo), Yorba Linda (in the hills north of Anaheim Hills), and North Huntington Beach. Each had its own unique challenges and joys. Central to it all were the many wonderful people who came and formed the nucleus of a new congregation, and whose stories we hold dear in our memories.

Two churches sent volunteers weekly to do canvassing of the neighborhoods in Rancho Santa Margarita on behalf of our project: Church of the Master in Mission Viejo and Irvine Presbyterian Church. Also working with us in this regard was Michael Regele, who provided the demographic information and direction necessary for our use. He was the founder and author of *Your Church and Its Mission (YCAIM)*, a process for mission self-study and action which was adopted by our presbytery for the use of all our churches. Another key person who joined us in this cooperative effort was Barbara Murphy who served on the staff of our presbytery as associate. She had been the director of Christian education at Tustin Presbyterian Church when I was their interim pastor, and at the presbytery we had the opportunity to work together again, this time in matters of church development, specifically with new and redeveloping racial/ethnic churches.

In the course of fulfilling my mission in church development, I realized that I needed more training than what I already had. Consequently, I enrolled in the Doctor of Ministry program at McCormick Theological Seminary, Chicago. My area of concentration was group organizational structure, conflict management, and the role of a presbytery executive.

It was a year-long study program. The professor from the seminary came to a group of us, in the same area of concentration, in the Southwest (usually Albuquerque, New Mexico) for a series of one week of intensive lecture/study sessions. We finally studied on campus for two weeks and worked on finalizing and defending our thesis. On June 7, 1991, I received the DMin degree. When people started addressing me as "Dr. Kassouni," my response was, "I'm still a patient, not a doctor." Maintaining the frame of mind of a student has kept me growing all the time, while also applying my knowledge to address issues at hand.

Stories Worth Remembering

There are a number of human-interest stories that are precious to us. They provide a peek into the dimension of human drama in new church development:

In conjunction with our Laguna Niguel project, developers offered us their office, a mobile building, since they had completed their objective and no longer had any use for it. We jumped at the offer and accepted it without first looking carefully at what was involved. We thought we could have it moved to the next project site, Rancho Santa Margarita, and use it as our center there. However, we discovered that it could not be moved that easily. The structure was not a mobile building after all, but a regular stucco-walled house. Consequently, the movers informed us that because of that fact, the cost of moving was going to be vastly higher than anticipated.

After swallowing that bitter pill, we then learned that moving it onto the new site in Rancho Santa Margarita was not possible because legal restrictions did not allow it. So, we were stuck with a mobile house on our hands. After having it moved to several temporary locations, we had it moved onto the back lot of our Japanese Presbyterian Church in Garden Grove. After a number of weeks there, the church informed us that it should be moved again. We just did not know where to have it moved again. It had turned into one big white elephant!

Thankfully, Christ Presbyterian Church of Huntington Beach, which was in a facilities-expansion program, offered to take it off our hands and use it as their administration center. However, that was easier said than done. We discovered that someone had moved in and made himself comfortable and was refusing to leave. Gary Watkins, pastor of Christ Presbyterian Church, volunteered to go and talk to the man. He reported to me that when he did so, the occupant not only refused to leave but threw a milk-carton full of urine on him! Well, the man finally relented when the police were called and took charge of the matter. Thus ended a very costly and scary project of ours.

In Rancho Santa Margarita, the presbytery had bought seven acres for our new church development. It was a parcel from a forty-acre site made available when the former owners could not hold on to it for lack of funds. It was the site the Saddleback Church originally had tried to buy but failed to keep up the payments. At the time Saddleback Church was using temporary quarters, renting the Trabuco High School in Mission Viejo.

Their pastor, the now-famous Rick Warren, called me.

"Kass, why don't we go together and build both yours and our churches on the site? We've claimed that land in faith for the location of our church."

"I think it is too late for that, Rick," I replied. "But I'll call the developer and see what can be done."

So I called the developer and said that it was Rick's dream to build there.

"Too late," he said. "The parcels have been sold already. I'm sorry for Rick, but sometimes dreams die hard."

Well, Rick and his people did not give up. They moved a few miles south and settled on a much better location where they built their famous church center. His dream was realized after all with a slight adjustment for location. Well, that's how close we came to growing a church in partnership with Saddleback Church!

Time Off for Studies in Israel/Palestine

In the spring of 1995, I took a month off for continuing studies. Samira joined me for one week at the conclusion of formal studies, for further travels together. Her focus was to find the house where she was born in the ancient city of Jaffa, south of Tel Aviv. Her father, the Rev. Dr. Farid Audeh, was the pastor of the Episcopal Church there at that time. Even though I had been to the Holy Land on a number of occasions, it was always mostly as a tourist.

Wanting to do some serious studies in Israel/Palestine, I attended St. George's College in Jerusalem. It was a continuing studies program of the Cathedral Church of St. George the Martyr, the Episcopal Cathedral in Jerusalem. The Most Rev. Samir Kafity was the bishop then. I registered for a one-month course titled "The Bible and the Holy Land," which included five days in the Sinai. Beyond facts, figures, stories, and biblical studies, what really captured my mind and soul were the variety of field trips we took in the country at large, along with our experiences in the Old City of Jerusalem. In our class of some twenty people, we had a variety of students from America and other countries, including a young Baptist pastor from north-eastern India.

Having been granted permission by the WAQF (Muslim governing council of their holy sites), we were allowed to enter places usually forbidden to tourists. We were given special tours of the Al Aqsa Mosque and the Dome of the Rock, built on the place where Solomon's Temple was originally located. What gripped my attention was what lay under the courtyard, beneath the structures above. We were invited to descend a stairway in a corner of the yard. As we did so, we encountered some men and women occupying a nook along our descent. They had built a makeshift mosque. The rationale was that by doing so they maintained their claim that not only the buildings above, but the ground beneath was Muslim holy ground, thus preventing their takeover by the Israeli government.

Continuing our descent, we arrived at a huge subterranean hall with many columns holding up the ceiling (the courtyard above). Tradition has it that it was originally used to keep the hundreds of horses belonging to King Solomon and later for storage at various times for a variety of purposes. Knowing how controversial this place was, with Orthodox Jews hoping to reclaim it, and the Muslims equally determined not allow that to happen, one can only imagine what probably is stored in that place.

The Church of the Holy Sepulcher is the focal point in Jerusalem for Christian identity. Again, apart from the well-known and documented aspects of that magnificent edifice, we were given a private visit of the deep subterranean room where Jesus's cross was discovered by St. Catherine, the mother of Emperor Constantine. We saw ancient graffiti on the walls left there by visitors of days gone by. Among them was the most captivating one, a drawing of a sailboat with the inscription in Latin, "LORD WE HAVE COME." It is interpreted to mean the pilgrims had come by boat, and by its design probably from Scandinavia. We all also whispered that prayer silently in that most holy place.

Among our many field trips, the outstanding and out of the way one was to Mt. Sinai, in the southern Negev desert. Our destination was St. Catherine's Monastery at the foot of the mountain, followed by our walk up to the top. The first night out we slept on the ground, under a canopy of stars. Our food was lamb roasted on an open fire pit by Bedouins. The idea was for us to catch the feel of the Israelites who were in that desert for forty years. The sun beat down on us, and we had no other place to find shade than among the rocky outcroppings around us. I then understood why the Psalmist often mentions "the cleft of the rock" as a place of shelter.

The second day we arrived at the Monastery, which has been in operation continually since it was initially founded around AD 330 by St. Catherine. It is built on the spot where Moses (it is claimed) saw the burning bush. Inside this magnificent fortress is a well where we were shown a bush growing. Yes, that is supposed to be it!

We saw some other sights worth remembering. One was a huge room full of bones, an ossuary, which contained the bones of all the monks of the past. What caught our attention was a platform at the end of the room, and there, sitting on a throne in full ecclesiastical regalia, was the skeleton of a highly revered Bishop of many years gone by!

They have two centers of religious worship there. The main one is the Greek Orthodox church containing many highly precious icons, one of which is claimed to be the oldest existing icon of Jesus. The other building is a small mosque. When news of Mohammed's advances north was received, they were very wise to build that mosque. In the narthex of the church there is a display, under glass, of important documents concerning their history. One very precious document is a letter from Mohammed instructing his armies not to destroy this monastery for two reasons: one, because the story of Moses was central to it, since, they, too revered Moses as a prophet; and second, because of the existence of the mosque in one corner of the complex.

This monastery is where Count Tischendorf in 1844 found an ancient set of manuscripts, the Septuagint (Greek) version of the Hebrew Bible, now called Codex Sinaiticus. He bought that and other ancient manuscripts, which the monks were using for fuel to fire up their ovens! These manuscripts are among the oldest in existence today and are housed in the British Museum in London.

At 3:00 a.m. we got up to start our journey to the top of the mountain called in Arabic *Jebel Mousa* (Moses's Mountain). It rises five thousand feet above sea level. They had secured camels for our use, and each of us mounted a camel (a first for me!) for this uphill climb of over a thousand feet. With a Bedouin guide walking alongside, mostly to make sure I did not fall off, we slowly ascended the mountain. It was the most uncomfortable ride on an animal I have ever had. The saddle kept shifting, and I was sure I'd fall off at any moment. Short of the peak, we stopped and walked the remaining several hundred feet. In complete silence we reached the top. We then gathered around a big flat stone where Holy Communion was prepared by our Anglican leader. We proceeded to celebrate the Eucharist just as the sun rose over the magnificent valley below us. It was for me what Rudolf Otto in his book *The Idea of the Holy* calls "a numinous moment," when the holy impacts our soul and spirit, leaving us speechless. Every time I read the verse, "Be still and know that I am God," I remember that awe-inspiring holy experience on Mt. Sinai. For several moments we prayed, we meditated, and we gazed in silence at that magnificent scene spread before us.

From there we began to walk down the mountain, all the way to the monastery. No more camels! I kept looking at the stones strewn along the way. When someone asked what I was looking for, my reply (in jest of course) was that ancient stones interested me, and one never knew what one could find in a place like this. Since it was here that Moses broke the first set of tablets of the Ten Commandments, I thought I might spot a fragment or two of it. I've always been an archeologist at heart, and since childhood have loved to explore. Cyprus, after all, is one huge pile of ancient ruins and a destination for many archeologists.

There were other field trips which were also very educational and inspiring. These included a trip to Masada, the mountaintop community that held out against the invading Roman armies after Jerusalem was captured in AD 70. Refusing to surrender, they chose instead mass suicide. That inspiring story is held sacred by Israel today. I understand all aspiring Israeli military cadets are brought there where they take their oath of allegiance and service. Most fascinating were the ruins of Qumran village and the caves where the Dead Sea Scrolls were found. Existing nearby was where the Essenes, a messianic community, was located. The possibility that John the Baptist may have been among the devotees of that commune, from where he came to the Jordan River heralding the coming of Christ, has been for me a significant historical link between the Old and New Testaments. Of course, we could not leave that area without going to the Dead Sea and testing the waters by floating in it for several minutes. We took special care that no water got into our eyes, because the minerals in the water would cause great harm. In these memoirs, I have been intentionally selective in sharing my experiences and trips during my studies in Israel. I have chosen those that have been personally most meaningful and those whose impact have spoken deeply to my soul.

After my studies had ended on June 27, Samira joined me for an extra week of travels together. First, I introduced her to the Rev. Dr. Canon Naim Ateek, pastor of the Palestinian Congregation of St. George's. He was the founder of SABEEL, a center for the study and promotion of Palestinian liberation theology. When I introduced her to him, he excitedly pulled up an old photo and showed it to her. It was of his father, Stifan Ateek, and Samira's father Farid walking together back in the 1940s, and there walking between them was little Naim. Those were the days when her father was a pastor of the Episcopal Church in Nazareth, and once a month he would go to their village called Beisan (Beth Shean today) to preach and lead them in worship.

We rented a car (with Israeli license plates) and started our trip in Jaffa (Joppa in the Bible), the ancient city south of Tel Aviv which is mostly Arab in population. Our reason for doing so was that it was where Samira was born, and she very much wished for us to find the house and also the church her father pastored. We found the Episcopal Church, but it was fenced with a padlock on the gate. We rattled the fence, called for someone to come, and after several minutes a boy appeared. He said the church was no longer used, and his parents were the hired caretakers. His instructions were to let no one in. After long pleadings we could see it was of no use to continue, and so we left. We went looking for her birthplace and thought we found the building, but we could not ascertain that for sure. We walked around town and saw the marked difference between this city and others, such as Tel Aviv, which was modern, clean, and shining, while Jaffa was drab, old, and noisy.

Haifa, a seaport at the foot of Mount Carmel, was our next destination, for her dad had been the pastor there also. We found the building, but we were told that it also sat empty except for funerals and weddings for the families that still lived there. Next we went looking for the buildings which once housed several families we knew back in America. Following the descriptions given to us by Stanley Khouri, whose father had been a prominent physician there before they all immigrated, we found the street and located the house, after a lot of questioning of local residents. However, we became increasingly uneasy. Because of our many inquiries and picture taking, we noticed that people were beginning to look at us with growing suspicion. So we stopped our inquiries and left.

A good place to go from there was the beach. When we arrived we found a vast expanse of sand with permanent canopies placed to provide shade. We remarked at how clean it was and the amazing fact that all the amenities, including parking, were offered free of charge. "Why can't we have this in America?" Samira wondered aloud.

"Maybe it's because Israel receives at least three billion dollars in aid from the United States every year, and some of it is being put to good use," I sarcastically replied.

We drove on to Nazareth in northern Galilee. This is one city where there is still a sizable number of Christians. They are mostly Roman Catholic and Greek Orthodox. Their influence is clearly displayed with a huge and beautiful church edifice called the Church of the Annunciation, built in 1969 at a cost of over $5 million, and is the largest Christian church in the Middle East. It is built over the grotto/caves where they believe the home of the Virgin Mary was located, and the place where she is believed to have been visited by the angel announcing that she was to be the mother of Jesus (the Annunciation, hence the church of that name situated above it).

The Episcopal Church there is open and doing quite well. This was the parish of Rev. Audeh's where Samira's sisters, Mona and Samia, were born. From here they moved to Jaffa, and then to Haifa. In 1947 he and the family relocated to Beirut, Lebanon. They left as the war for Israel's independence was imminent. Samira was only four at the time.

The Rev. Canon Riah Abu El Assal, pastor of the church, remembered Rev. Audeh well and spoke of him with highest regard. He showed us around and took us to the house where the Audeh family lived. It was being used as an extended facility for the church's education program.

Located on high ground overlooking the old city, the church owned and operated a lovely hostel called St. Margaret's, where we stayed several nights. It was a pleasure to open the windows at night and let the cool breezes in. However, it also was in a position where we could hear all the noises emanating from the city below. In the middle of the night the call of the muezzin sounded from the minarets (Each mosque has a tower called a minaret) calling the faithful to prayer. We counted five of them, each starting several minutes after another had ended. Upon our inquiry as to why that was so, we were told that each wanted to keep his call distinguished from the others. What added to our misery was that all the dogs in town were awakened because of it, and their howling prevented us from going back to sleep! Their barking was followed by the call of the roosters announcing the coming dawn. O Nazareth, we will not forget you!

I had read so much about the kibbutzim (collective farms and communities) established in Israel by their early settlers, and I wanted to visit one. This we did by driving to the south-eastern shore of Lake Galilee, also called Kinneret, or Tiberias. It was Kibbutz Ein-Gev, established as one of the oldest in Israel, dating back to the 1930s. It is mostly a tourist center now, catering to tourists and vacationers. We found a grassy area and stretched out on the lawn to rest and enjoy the scenery with boats sailing and people swimming and enjoying themselves. After just ten or so minutes, we noticed all the boats coming in for safe harbor. Winds had picked up and were getting stronger and stronger. Waves began to crash against the shore, and we had to evacuate to higher ground. We had a perfect eye-witness experience of what happened when the disciples were crossing the lake, with Jesus asleep in the boat. The winds suddenly came up and they cried, "Lord, wake up for we perish!" It is located in the Rift Valley, a fissure in the earth's crust stretching from Syria to central Africa. Lake Tiberias (Galilee) is almost seven hundred feet below sea level. This phenomenon of nature has created a huge funnel like indentation through which winds often come howling down from the north. We witnessed it, and it was awesome!

In the city of Tiberias, on the western shores of the lake, we stayed in the Guest House, part of the Sea of Galilee Center, sponsored by the

Church of Scotland and Episcopal Church in Jerusalem. St. Andrew's Church is also located in that center. This is a historic place because it was a hospital for many years, the first in the area, founded by Dr. David Torrance over one hundred years ago. We walked the grounds, close by the shores, and read a number of names of missionaries past who are buried in a small cemetery there.

I was quite interested in their story because in America the Presbyterian Church has its roots in the Church of Scotland. Talking with their pastor in Jerusalem, I learned about this center, and that together they formed the presbytery. In answer to my inquiry concerning the number of church members they had, I was surprised to hear that it was around twenty-five in Jerusalem and around twelve in Tiberias. To me, it is a demonstration of what I said in the beginning of my memoirs, that we have been witnessing the end of an era in the Middle East, with the passing of churches and their institutions established in colonial times. No passing of the torch to locals, no evangelization, no transformation from a foreign to a local church. That's sad.

Lake Galilee has been the main source of water for the country. The Jordan River starts flowing from its southern tip and ends in the Dead Sea. In the sixty-five miles it travels, it drops down another eighteen hundred feet, before reaching the Dead Sea, which itself is the lowest point on the earth. The government has built a place for pilgrims to be baptized in this river. However, it is not just above the Dead Sea, as the Bible locates it (where John the Baptist baptized the early converts and also Jesus), but at the beginning of the river's flow. Just past this lush, green, and pleasant spot we came across huge pipes installed in the river, siphoning and pumping most of the water away to distribute to the inland and the southern deserts. As a result, very little water continues to flow down the Jordan. So today this river is but a mere shadow of its renowned self.

Before leaving the lake, we had our lunch at one of the many lakeside restaurants serving the legendary St. Peter's fish. We sat at a table on the deck of one such restaurant with a beautiful view. In addition to eating our fish (which, by the way, was nothing to brag about), we listened and engaged several people in conversation. At a table next to ours was an American-Jewish family with two little girls. They were being questioned by the father as to what they had seen and by what they had been impressed on their trip. What caught our attention (especially Samira's) was the father's observation with emphasis: "This land was a desert till our people came, and now it is a beautiful garden."

Samira almost, but not quite, was ready with her response: "There was no lake here until then?"

We had an interesting conversation with an elderly couple, who proceeded to tell us they were leaving Israel after many years of living there and working in the development of kibbutzim. "Israel has changed," they said. "It is not what we pioneers envisioned. Materialism has replaced our ideals, and the new generation has no place for what we have cherished here."

From there we drove south, paralleling the Jordan River. Our trip to Bethlehem was extraordinary. We had already met Rev. Bishara Awad, president of Bethlehem Bible College, who had advised us not to drive into Bethlehem with a car bearing Israeli license plates (as ours was). The Bible College's main building was deeded to them by Danish missionaries, who used to have a hospital there. Dr. Awad invited us to drive to the college, less than a mile outside the city, and park there. He would then drive us to central Bethlehem and pick us up sometime later in the day. The reason for this arrangement was that our car would be vandalized if we were to park in the city with the Israeli plates. Taking his advice, we drove to the college first. It was a remarkable place which had become, under his guidance, a center for both Arabs and Jews to study the Bible. We actually met a group of Jews and Arabs studying together. This was for us a demonstration of their emphasis on reconciliation. It is expressed in the Arabic word *Musalaha*, the name of a peace-making program there, meaning forgiveness and reconciliation. Dr. Awad drove us to the main square in Bethlehem. On one side was the Church of the

Nativity, and across the square was the mosque, and in between a tower with Israeli soldiers keeping their eyes on everything going on below.

I immediately noticed something odd, in comparison with previous visits I'd made there. We walked into the Church, and we were the only people there. Where were the usual crowds? In former visits, we used to stay in line waiting to get in through the tiny opening of a doorway in this fortress-like building. But not today. Our question was answered after we had walked through and prayed in silence at the little grotto with a silver star signifying the spot where tradition says Jesus was born. It was almost noon by then when a guide walked up to us.

"Come with me to one of the gift shops and wait there," he said. "Today is Friday, and the men are in the mosque for prayers. When they come out at noon they will start demonstrating against the Israeli occupation. This happens every Friday. After an hour they will all quiet down and go home. Then business will go on as usual."

From the safety of the gift shop, full of carved olive-wood souvenirs, we waited, camera and video recorder ready. Sure enough at noon, the men came pouring out of the mosque shouting, gesturing, and throwing bottles in protest against the occupation. After an hour the square was empty again. Something fascinating then took place. A caravan of limousines drove up to the Church and stopped. From the lead car out stepped a bride, dressed in a gorgeous white wedding dress, and the groom in his black tuxedo. Followed by scores of people in their party, they all went into the Church for the wedding ceremony. What a contrast between this and the former scene! We thus got a dramatic, and quite surreal, example of how the people had adjusted to the realities of their political condition and were surviving against great odds.

Through it all the Israeli soldiers were watching, with no apparent agitation at what was going on below. Tourists and others soon came back to the square, and life assumed its usual hustle and bustle. The words of the carol came to mind, "O little town of Bethlehem, how still we see thee lie." It's not very still any longer. Just a few years later, the soldiers left, and the tower came down. But in its place a twenty-foot-high ugly cement wall has been built surrounding the city, with a check point for all going in and coming out. It now takes several hours for the trip that took us only half an hour from Jerusalem.

We left the country with extremely mixed emotions, especially so when Samira was taken aside at the airport in Tel Aviv and questioned for over an hour. Who was she really? How was it that she was born in Jaffa, was travelling with an American passport, married to an Armenian from Cyprus, with travel plans to go to Cyprus and then to Beirut? What kind of work did she do in America? Finally, quite irritated and exhausted, she said, "I teach your children, who leave Israel and come to California, how to speak English!"

With that said, we were allowed to proceed on our flight to Cyprus. My resolve is never to return to Israel unless and until that ugly wall is removed! I have not seen it, and I don't care to see it ever. I am waiting for an American president, someday soon, who will dare to go to Jerusalem, stand beneath that ugly wall, and cry out, "Mr. Netanyahu, tear down this wall!"

In August 1995, we returned from our Middle East trip and resumed our respective duties: Samira to her teaching, and I to my ministry with Los Ranchos Presbytery, with its variety of projects and challenges.

Speaking in Tongues

A significant portion of my work involved coming alongside racial/ethnic churches and assisting them to grow. The nationalities in this list included: Hispanic/Latino, Korean, Chinese, Vietnamese, Cambodian, and Japanese congregations. Each was unique with needs different from the others, requiring special attention. In many ways my being Armenian helped, since I also was an immigrant to this country and understood their struggles. My main observation was that most of them did not really understand the Presbyterian way of worship and were ill at ease with its formality and church government. However, they hung in there for the financial support they were getting year after year. It was my observation that if things continued in that way, many of them would not survive.

One church in East Los Angeles, called El Siloe Presbyterian Church is a good case in point. The presbytery bought the land and paid for a church facility totaling hundreds of thousands of dollars (financed by our MOOD program). The salary of the pastor and church budget were largely underwritten by the presbytery. It was my assignment to meet with the pastor and help him develop evangelism programs to reach people in the neighborhood and invite them to the church. He resented my interference in his way of doing things and refused, claiming that his TV program was evangelism outreach enough. Eventually, after some twenty years, the congregation dwindled to the point that it became obvious to all that it was no longer viable. The church was closed, and the building was eventually sold. That which began with a glorious ground-breaking service ended up quietly in failure.

There were success stories also. Grace Presbyterian Church was a Japanese/American church located in Long Beach. It was not a new church, having been in existence for over fifty years. They were a self-supporting congregation but had a big problem. Their membership had dwindled. The remaining loyal few continued to come to their church located in old Long Beach, across from a public bathhouse, which was one reason they wanted to relocate. They were survivors of the internment of Japanese Americans during World War II, and while they were away their building was mostly abandoned and looted. There was a sense of gloom among them, with not much hope for their future.

In 1992, when I began to meet with them to see what could be done, I discovered that they had close to $50,000 in savings but no pastor. After much prayer and consultation, they agreed to a plan we suggested, which comprised of three points: first, move to a new location; second, call a full-time pastor; and third, use their savings along with the income from the sale of their building to finance the salary of the pastor and church budget for at least one year. If things did not work out, then they would disband, and the church would close. The toughest part was the first. Where would they or could they go? They approached a sister Presbyterian church, the Community Presbyterian Church of Long

Beach, with a request to move in with them. But they were turned down, with anti-Japanese sentiment expressed in the congregational meeting called to consider their request. Gloom was thickening, and they were growing desperate.

While driving my car one day, an idea hit me and grew stronger and stronger. Faith Presbyterian Church in Paramount, a few miles north of Long Beach, was an Anglo congregation with just a handful of people left. The church was going to close. We approached them with the proposal that Grace Church could possibly come and use their facility. They and the presbytery agreed to it. We then presented the idea to the Japanese congregation, and they, too, agreed.

The next big hurdle was to locate and call a pastor willing to take on the challenge. Haroldine Chandler, the wife of our executive presbyter, agreed to do the demographic studies needed to convince a candidate that this church could have a very good future, since there were so many Japanese Americans in Orange County.

The candidate for the position of pastor we focused on was a recent graduate of Princeton Seminary. He had many questions about the viability of this congregation and our collective vision for its future. He was finally convinced and agreed to take on the challenge. His name was the Rev Steve Yamaguchi, a Japanese American born in California. He was the right choice. Excitement and membership grew with his coming. They moved to Paramount and thrived there. Several years ago they decided to merge with Long Beach Lakewood First Presbyterian Church, and create together an international church. After serving several years as their co-pastor with the Rev. Steve Wirth, Steve Yamaguchi was chosen to be the new executive presbyter of Los Ranchos Presbytery, after the resignation of Rev. David Tomlinson, who had followed John Chandler following his retirement.

A New Life with Samira

1. Wedding day for Vartkes and Samira Kassouni. First Presbyterian Church, Santa Ana, California, December 20, 1987.
2. Samira Audeh Kassouni.
3. The happy couple.
4. Our home for thirty years in Orange, California.

My Education Continues

Continuing education time at St. George Cathedral, Jerusalem, with fellow student, Rev. K. Somi Nagaland of India, 1995.

Doctor of Ministry degree received at McCormick Seminary, Chicago, Illinois, June 7, 1991.

Celebrating with me were *(left to right)* wife Samira, sister-in-law Olivette, and brother Sarkis.

Travels in Cyprus

1. Remnants of the Armenian Evangelical community gathered for worship in the Greek Evangelical Church, led by Dr. Hrayr Jebejian *(back. center)*. Nicosia, Cyprus, April 2011.
2. Dr. Hrayr Jebejian and me.
3. Dedication of my father's biography (Dr.Yervant Kassouny, author), Archbishop Varoujan Hergelian, officiating. Nicosia, Cyprus, April 11, 2011.
4. My sister, Nouvart, was honored with a special recognition of her many services to the Armenian community at the same gathering.

Renowned artist Vartan Tashjian in his studio with Samira and me.

A special gift, a painting of my home church in Larnaca, Cyprus, by the artist.

Nine

Retiring but Not Tiring

The year 1996 was a pivotal one for me. First, I resigned from my position in Los Ranchos Presbytery, freeing me up to accept new pastoral assignments on an interim basis, taking me all over Orange County and San Fernando Valley. That same year I also retired legally, making me eligible to start drawing my pension from the Pensions Board. Being sixty-five meant little to me in the sense that I was still physically healthy, mentally alert, and highly motivated to carry on and not be put out to pasture. However, I also remembered my response to a colleague of mine, who was being urged to retire. He said, "Ministers do not retire, they only re-tire or retread and go on rolling."

"Yes, but even retreads go flat sometimes," I replied, cautioning him that we must be careful and aware that our pride can prevent us from seeing our limitations due to advancing years. Keeping this cautionary word in mind, I took on the new opportunities for service presented to me. So, since I'm not tired or burned out, I've coined the phrase "not tiring."

My first postretirement call was to the First Presbyterian Church of Garden Grove. This historic church was organized in 1952 by the Rev. Dr. Tom Gillespie, who served as their pastor during the years considered their glory days. He had gone on eventually to become the president of Princeton Seminary. Those were years of booming growth for Presbyterians across the land. And it was no different in southern California. Membership grew to over two thousand, and a beautiful church edifice was built with Dr. Gillespie's leadership.

Today the building stands as a silent witness to the steady decline of our denomination. Demographic changes, migration of members to new communities in southern California, inability to maintain a strong evangelistic program, and theological disputes mirroring the controversies raging in the PC(USA) have contributed to the decline of this church. Membership was less than three hundred when I took on the task of being their interim pastor.

Samira joined me in this challenging and yet rewarding ministry. Being an educator by profession, in addition to her gift of hospitality, she and I teamed up to address our opportunities.

My primary task was to help bring healing in the congregation that was suffering from controversy regarding their former minister. He had resigned after a short period and left the church in turmoil. My calling as pastor was put to use right away, providing attention and loving service so vital to the remaining members.

We also began to focus attention on a possible source of new growth: the Vietnamese Presbyterian Church that was using the facility for their needs. This was the first Vietnamese church of Presbyterian connection in all of America. What a grand opportunity this was for us all. Instead of considering them merely as being renters, or nesters, we met together to consider points of shared ministry, with the vision that someday we could merge our congregations.

Since we had an active Sunday school, but with few students, and they had many children who would benefit from an English language program, we agreed to merge into one Sunday school, with Samira as their organizer. This experiment did not last long, however, due to differences in cultures, language, and lack of sufficient students on our part.

When we were living in Los Angeles, the name Garden Grove conjured up in my mind an idyllic city with groves and gardens throughout, but in reality it is far different. Where orchards of oranges once thrived, today there are houses, buildings, and shopping centers. Latinos and Vietnamese have replaced white Anglo-Saxons, who have moved farther south creating new communities. The few who are still there are bravely trying to keep their church going, but to me it is a heroic yet seemingly hopeless endeavor.

From Garden Grove to San Fernando Valley

San Fernando Presbytery was composed of thirty-five churches, spanning from Westlake Village in the west to Glendale in the east. I was called to be their interim executive presbyter in 1999, and I served them for two years in that capacity.

Controversy over the issue of the ordination of homosexual people was beginning to embroil our churches, and especially so with us because the retiring executive, whom I was following, was gay, and he made no effort to hide it. On the contrary, he promoted it openly. This issue, coupled with that of changing ethnic neighborhoods and declining church membership, presented me with quite a challenge.

Samira and I discussed the prospect of my commuting from Orange to Panorama City (seventy miles away, where the offices were located). We agreed that commuting daily would be crazy. Consequently, I sought from among our constituent members a home where I could rent a room or two during the week for five days, and then go home over the weekends. My search was quickly rewarded with an invitation from a couple in Encino who had a guest house on their property and offered it for my use. It was a Godsend indeed. This arrangement worked out very well, and for two years it became my headquarters.

The highlight of my service in San Fernando Presbytery was a presbytery-wide mission study including all the churches. It was an attempt to help us determine the key role of the presbytery; to help member churches review their life, individually and in relation to other Presbyterian churches in proximity to them; and together to vision their future. It was the first time that they had gotten involved in such an endeavor, and consequently a number felt threatened by it. However, one cluster of churches in the Burbank area took it seriously, and we met together weekly for a number of weeks. The tangible result was that one church, Bethany Presbyterian, began serious talks with First Presbyterian. Within a few weeks they agreed to discontinue as a separate church and unite their assets and membership with First Presbyterian for a strong presence in Burbank and a future together in mission.

Concurrent with my ministry and church-related work, I maintained connections with friends outside of the churches. High on the list in this regard were Bhisham and Binoo Bakhshi, and their two sons, who were introduced to my readers in chapter 4. After years of silence, we reconnected in the mid '80s. Somehow he had tracked me down after a long search. After sharing our old memories of times together, he opened up his heart to me. His two grown sons had been in America and completed their college education. Since he and Binoo lived in India, he wondered whether I would stay in touch with them and help out as may be needed. For almost twenty years, I was involved in one way or another, growing close to them all. From time to time, Bhisham and then Binoo would come to Los Angeles to be with them, and we would get together. In the course of their visits, we talked a lot with each other about life, values, and religion. In the course of it all, Bhisham and I grew very close, like brothers, and my admiration of him increased.

The Bakhshis were high-caste Hindu Brahmins who followed their faith openly, and without excuses. He and I became like brothers, sharing our thoughts without hesitation or judgmental attitude. For me, the climactic moment in our talks came when one day he pulled out a paper out of his pocket and said, "Here, read this, it is my favorite poem." To my great surprise it was our favorite hymn, "Amazing Grace"! He had a positive view of Christianity and of Jesus.

"Are you saying to me that you affirm this song when it says, 'Amazing grace how sweet the sound, that saved a wretch like me. I once was lost but not I'm found. Was blind but now I see,'" I asked.

"Yes, I do" was his reply.

I knew he was doing this without his rejection of Hinduism. I knew that Hindus, who are in a way syncretists, often do include Jesus in the list of deities whom they venerate, but this was different. There was a witness of the Spirit to me, that here was a child of God, "saved by grace" just like me.

This amazing man, who had risen to the highest ranks in the Indian government as head of the Indian Oil Company, was a humble and self-effacing man. He had traveled widely and knew the Middle East well. He knew Islam so well that in Baalbeck when he was detained by Hezbollah soldiers, they not only released him a few hours later, but gave him a tour of the famous ruins. They did so because he talked to them so convincingly that they thought he was Muslim! He knew Christianity and lived according to Jesus's teachings. He believed that Jesus's silent years were lived in India. He gave me a book by Holger Kersten, a German scholar, titled *Jesus Lived in India* (Penguin Books, 2001). I've read it with great interest indeed.

Bhisham has been for me a living link between me and the unknown, and ignored, mysterious India and the Far East. I say this to my own shame, because I have hardly bothered to absorb wisdom and culture emanating from there. He often urged us to travel to India, and we always put it off. Even though I was there in 1969, I really did not connect with the people. Now that he is departed from us, I feel that our opportunity to do so has slipped away.

Back to Orange County

Following my work in San Fernando, I served several churches as interim pastor. These were Geneva Presbyterian Church of Laguna Hills, Yorba Linda Presbyterian Church, and Morningside Presbyterian Church in Fullerton. Each was unique with special challenges. Geneva Presbyterian, with around one thousand members had had a very noteworthy growth under the leadership of Rev. Michael Wenning. He had moved on to Bel Aire Presbyterian in Los Angeles, a very well-known church which included President and Mrs. Ronald Reagan in its membership. He was the minister who officiated at President Reagan's funeral service in 2004. Our ministry there was very well received with enthusiasm, and spiritual vitality was clearly evident in all areas of its life. Their associate pastor, Tom Cramer, continued to serve with me, and we developed a very close and lasting friendship. Several years later he went on to be the co-executive presbyter at Los Ranchos Presbytery.

There were several significant ministries at the Geneva church. One was their contemporary service every Saturday night, which drew many involved in the thriving youth program there. Key to it was the excellent music program, under the direction of the Stark brothers. I loved to be part of their service, bringing the message from the Word every week. In all the churches I have attended, theirs has been the one with the highest quality of performance and audience participation. Also, their Christian Education program was exceptional. I have always emphasized adult-level education in all the churches I have served, but this one was special. I taught a number of classes with a focus on biblical studies and related subjects. Attendance in those classes was always excellent, numbering between fifty and one hundred.

A highlight of my ministry at Geneva was a one-week men's retreat we had in Baja, California, at the summer cabin owned by Tom Cramer's family. In preparation for it, we all read Karen Armstrong's book *The Battle for God*[3] and then spent that whole week discussing its highly relevant contents dealing with fundamentalism in Judaism, Christianity, and Islam. This provided an excellent orientation to help us understand the religious and political upheavals in these faiths, especially that of Islam in the Middle East. Another innovative thing we did there was to start a monthly "Discussion of Contemporary Issues." The subjects were social, political, scientific, and cultural matters. The presenters were people with knowledge and experience in their respective topics. We attempted

---

3 *The Battle for God*, Karen Armstrong, Ballantine Books, New York, 2001

to create a time and a place where we could consider controversial subjects without fear of stepping outside the bounds of traditional religious and cultural belief systems.

Geneva had a plan already adopted for the expansion of their facilities. They envisioned a new chapel next to their existing magnificent sanctuary, the addition of an elevator in their education building, and a complete redoing of their courtyard. All this would cost them around $2 million, with half of it in hand already. To lead the effort to raise the extra million was a challenge presented to me, which we took on in faith. By the time we ended our ministry there, the new facilities were built and in full operation.

Geneva had been built on land donated by the developers of Laguna Woods, a planned community for seniors. Many people from there and the vicinity of the church were members. Among them was Jean Brokaw, the mother of Tom Brokaw, of TV and literary fame. In my visits with her, I gained much knowledge and insight into his person. It was my hope that we could get him to come and speak to our congregation at a special function. I corresponded with him, and he agreed to come sometime in the future. However the year 2002 being a presidential election year, he was very busy and wished to postpone his coming. Well, since my ministry there would soon end, I could not pursue the matter any further, and he never did come.

Yorba Linda Presbyterian Church, in the city of Yorba Linda, had been the third in our new church development program back in the late 1980s. Little did I ever think that I would return there as their stated supply pastor. This designation is different from that of interim pastor; in churches where there is conflict and serious problems, the presbytery assigns a pastor to deal with the situation. In this case I was asked to go there because I had been their initiating pastor and had knowledge of their history. Samira and I had started that project by gathering a number of people in a house existing on the property and using it as our first meeting place.

Our assignment now was to not only preach, teach, and carry on a visitation program but most importantly to deal with the conflicts among the members and to address their present and future life, until calm prevailed. Only then would they move forward with the search process for a new pastor. In this case, there had been serious loss of confidence in their former pastor, and his resignation had been requested.

We labored there for two years. Several challenges regarding church staff and management of the office were addressed successfully. We had a very positive and rewarding time together. After notifying the presbytery that they were ready to move on to a search for their pastor, we left them with heavy hearts, knowing we could not continue beyond the fulfillment of the task that brought us there.

Morningside Presbyterian Church in Fullerton was a small church with less than two hundred members. Their original vision was to build a church in the bedroom communities surrounding California State University in Fullerton, which was newly established. However, the expected influx never did materialize. They had a big campus with ample space to build a sanctuary, which they never did because of lack of growth. Hence, they were using a large room in the Christian Education unit not intended for worship. What they had hoped would be temporary ended up being their permanent sanctuary.

My time among them as their interim pastor was from 2006 to 2008. They had a Korean congregation with a parallel worship and Sunday school program whose membership had been incorporated into the church's roll of members, and their pastor was considered to be an associate pastor. This had been done in the previous administration with the intention and dream of growing a multiethnic congregation. Well, things had not gone that way, and the cost involved in keeping the Korean pastor on the payroll was a challenge.

We developed a survey to see what the people (including the Koreans) envisioned their future to be. The upshot of it was that they resolved not to continue this relationship, and the Koreans whose numbers had dwindled to less than twenty, decided to leave. After this painful process for all involved, the congregation was ready to move forward unencumbered. They then proceeded to the next phase of searching for a pastor.

Among the people who worshipped with us were two men who came regularly. One day I was approached by one of them with a question and a request.

"Pastor Kass, we are very happy here and would wish to join the church. However, I have one question. Would you accept gays as members? The man I sit with in church is my partner, and the two children up front every Sunday are a boy and a girl we have adopted. Four of us live together as a family in a house we own near this church."

He went to tell me about themselves, and he shared with me his vibrant evangelical faith in Christ and history of going from church to church seeking acceptance and affirmation of themselves. He had tried every possible way to live as a heterosexual but failed, and he had contemplated suicide even.

This was a first for me, and I had never faced this kind of a situation before. However, I had studied the subject, and seriously thought and prayed as to what I would do if I were to face this situation. I was ready with my answer:

"My friend, I will approach our session with your request for membership and share your story with them. I will gladly recommend that they approve your request. If they refuse, I will resign my position as pastor right there. Jesus never refused his love of all who approached him. That's the good news of the Gospel."

He then proceeded with a second question:

"Our children have never been baptized. Would you baptize them"?

"I would do so gladly," I responded.

Instead of refusing his request, the session approved it unanimously. We proceeded to accept him and his partner as members and made plans for the baptism of their children. In doing so I was confronted with a dilemma. In the ceremony, who would come forward as their parents? On the morning of the sacrament, around a dozen members of their families were in church. When the time came for me to call the parents forward, I said, "I now call on family and friends to come forward and stand with this family and form a circle around these children." All their friends came forward and formed a circle of love around them. We then proceeded with the ceremony. It was a heart-warming demonstration of the love of Christ bringing us together, and a witness to his revolutionary grace in action. This family became strong leaders in the church, and their children became leaders of our youth group.

A heart-wrenching experience for me while serving this church in Fullerton, was to hear that a dear friend of mine, from many years back, was residing in a facility for people with Alzheimer's disease only a few blocks away from our church. Her nephew who lived in Fullerton had brought her there. Marge Young (Yeghoian) was a distant relative of mine, whom I had met in Philadelphia over fifty years before. She resided, with her father, in a house across the street from the Philadelphia branch of International Students Inc. (ISI), which I directed. In Fullerton I visited her weekly. She always remembered me, but much of her memory was gone. She kept wanting to drive home (or walk there if necessary) to Pasadena to be with her father, who had died many years before. She died a few months after I left the church, and I officiated at her funeral.

Our work having been completed in Fullerton, we moved to our next assignment. At that point it was my deep-felt conviction that I should not take on a full-time pastorate any longer.

Back to Tustin

In 1985 I had been invited to be the interim pastor of Tustin Presbyterian Church. I served there till early 1986. Now, in 2008, after a meeting with

Pastor Rebecca Prichard, I agreed to come on as their parish associate for visitation on a part-time basis. After twenty-two years I was back in Tustin. I had been received by them initially with much love and affirmation of my leadership. We had many fond memories as well as friendships that had lasted years of separation. We had maintained our residence in the area, and Samira had joined the church several years earlier. So it was a very natural fit for us. My primary duty was to make pastoral calls and visits with the members who were in hospitals or confined to their homes and with those who were having crises or challenges in their old age. I also participated in the worship services by bringing the pastoral prayers, sharing events in our life together, preaching from time to time, and teaching adult-level Bible classes.

One can hardly put on paper the profoundly meaningful, emotionally challenging, and intellectually stimulating times I've had at TPC. I watched and listened with empathy the struggle many were going through to maintain their health. I prayed with those who were facing their death. I shared tears with spouses and their families whose loved ones were gone. I shared biblical verses and insights concerning our common destiny in life and death in the grace of our Lord, Jesus Christ.

Meeting with a group of our men on Friday mornings, not as a pastor, but as one of them with equal questions and struggles in life as they, has been a precious experience for me. Listening to each one nonjudgmentally, joining in the conversation with no fear of being considered too liberal or too conservative, and standing in support of each other has been the source of much affirmation and strength for all of us.

Turmoil and Separation

Apart from life in the local congregation, I became active again in the Presbytery of Los Ranchos. There I began to observe the deliberate and disturbing trend toward separation, on the part of a number of member congregations from the presbytery and PC(USA). What had been in the earlier years a united and mutually loving presbytery was slowly but surely entering the abyss of division and alienation. This was not a new phenomenon. The Presbyterian Church, like all other denominations, has been embroiled in theological and political controversies for over a century. It began at the turn of the twentieth century with fights over issues of modernism versus fundamentalism. Litmus tests of all kinds have been promoted to ascertain what theological orthodoxy should look like.

This constant bickering, arguing, separating from one another, and forming new alliances to maintain purity of the faith has slowly eroded my own thinking concerning the claims of Protestantism in America. However, in my own personal convictions and spiritual growth, I have gone in the opposite direction that fundamentalists have taken. Led by God's Spirit, I have been freed up to have positive feelings about other churches, such as the Roman Catholic and Eastern Orthodox churches. This has been distinctly so in my relations with the Armenian Apostolic Church.

In 2014, after two years of what was called "Discernment Process," a significant number of our churches in Los Ranchos Presbytery decided to leave us and join a new denomination titled Evangelical Covenant Community of Presbyterians (ECO for short). A number of our prominent churches joined in the exodus. What a shame that after many years of working and worshiping together in harmony we came to this deplorable point. What has become obvious is that the pastor, or pastors, in each church played a key role. If they said, "Let us leave," the congregation left. If they said, "Let us not leave," the congregation stayed. It was clear to me that several pastors, who were new to our presbytery, came with their "baggage" filled with arguments criticizing the denomination and pressing for a final decision.

In June 2013, I wrote "An open letter to our pastors and churches," and mailed it to all clergy listed in our presbytery. Here is its content:

Dear brothers and sisters in Christ:

My letter to you comes rather late in the process called "Discernment" by the Presbytery of Los Ranchos. However, it comes with the sincere hope that you will consider the following points I raise in lieu of this process, before it is too late for us all to remain in the same room while we carry our times of prayer, discussion, and mission.

It is very obvious and glaringly clear that in most of our arguments calling for separation from the Los Ranchos Presbytery, and the PC(USA), we have ignored the mandate given to us by our Lord Jesus Christ, to "love one another." (John 13:34–36) Jesus emphasized that and amplified it by saying, "By this everyone will know that you are my disciples, if you love one another." The letters of John lift this up as being the uttermost in importance among all the matters confronting his readers. I have yet to hear or read from those advocating separation any serious focus on this teaching by Christ, the Lord of the Church!

One may argue, as is done often, that Jesus's call to unity is not in reference to the institutional or "monolithic" church, as represented by Los Ranchos Presbytery or our denomination. If this argument were to hold true, then allegiance to the local church, which you represent, is not also called for, which is also an institution. If so, then why do you not tolerate dissent and diversity within your own ranks? If you tolerate dissent and diversity in your own ranks as a local church, while maintaining spiritual unity, why then do you advocate separation on the Presbytery and national level? Shakespeare said, "Consistency, thou art a jewel."

The metaphor of the body and its members is quite suitable for the point I make. I hear members of the body saying to the body, and to some other members of the body, "We don't need you any longer. We will stick together so an arm can recognize an arm and a leg can recognize a leg, and feel good in our fellowship together. We don't need, and we reject those who do not look and act like us."(With apologies to Paul for this paraphrase of I Corinthians 12:14).

If we no longer recognize each other, with our differences, to be the body of Christ, then where will such unity in Christ continue visibly?

Churches have been splitting from each other for two thousand years. They have been excommunicating each other, as being heretics, for centuries. Consequently, the body has suffered dearly. In the Presbyterian Church we have had the Southern, the Northern, the United, the Reformed, the Orthodox, the Evangelical, on and on, with each claiming to have finally formed the true biblically authorized church! This is the scandal of the brokenness of the body of Christ which no one wishes or dares to address in our "discernment" process! This is the proverbial elephant in the room. Whether it be the particulars of sexual morality, doctrinal affirmations, or biblical interpretations, it is this matter which Jesus calls us to consider. I call on us to do so before it is too late, and the new affiliations, whether they be ECO or something else, separates us into new factions and the macabre dance continues to go on and on.

When I pledged allegiance to our church it was tantamount to my allegiance to Jesus Christ, because the Church is the body of Christ. An invisible Christ is easy to manipulate and form him in my own image. However, the church challenges me to change in the light of Christ's priorities and mandates which may not be acceptable to me in the light of my personal ideas, but change is called for nevertheless! This is what a "church reformed and always reforming" means.

I call upon our pastors and elders to lead our churches in the spirit of Christ, in this time of crisis among us. And in doing so let us remember what Paul said in 2 Corinthians 3:6, "The letter kills, but the Spirit gives life."

The turmoil within the churches at large has infected Armenian Evangelical churches also. Our own First Armenian Presbyterian Church of Fresno voted to leave our parent Presbyterian Church (USA) denomination in 2012 and join the Evangelical Presbyterian Church denomination, which is itself an offshoot of the PC(USA). When I got wind of the impending move, I called their pastor and registered my deep-felt sorrow concerning it. In doing so the church has lost its place of honor, its significant leadership role in the San Joaquin Presbytery, and its witness to the community at large. Its adoption of a fundamentalist position is evidenced by such decisions as the refusal to ordain women to the position of elder, thus abrogating a policy of inclusivism that had been in place for many years.

Another disturbing evidence of this trend back to fundamentalism is the unbelievable episode of the rejection and destruction of new hymnbooks by the Armenian Evangelical Union of North America (AEUNA) in the year 2010. Hrant and Lucina Aghbabian had been chosen and delegated the task of preparing a new bilingual Armenian Evangelical hymnbook, seventeen years before this sad event. They labored hard and long and produced a magnificent hymnal which was excellent in every way, except one. They made it gender inclusive in some, but not all hymns, and they also changed some, but not all, references to God in the masculine gender. After the AEUNA leadership had initially approved it, their position changed. Their new leadership took a very negative stand against its use, and consequently over three thousand copies were secretly shredded.

Eventually, this hymnbook was reprinted, after removing by agreement, all references to the AEUNA as sponsor. This was made possible by its new sponsor, the Armenian Heritage Committee of the Armenian Congregational Church of Detroit. Leading in this commendable effort was the Rev. Dr. Vahan Tootikian, pastor emeritus of the Detroit church, and chairman of the committee. He has been an immovable rock in the midst of shifting sands, in this and other issues concerning our churches.

Why all this conflict and confusion? Because of the reactionary nature of fundamentalism. It is based on the sadly mistaken notion that certain doctrines must be championed at all costs, for the sake of preserving the doctrinal purity of the Gospel. It is the same old battle of championing tradition over the freedom to move forward under the guidance of the Holy Spirit to address change. How ironic that going backward in the name of Christ is considered going forward in our witness to him. I have a saying that is relevant: Christ is always ahead of us, calling us to follow. He is not behind us calling us to retreat.

A number of us banded together, encouraged to do so by the Rev. Jirair Sogomian, former pastor of Immanuel Armenian Congregational Church of Downey. In the light of these developments, we decided in 2012 to start a website called ARMEVIEW (ARMENIAN EVANGELICAL REVIEW). The declared purpose was to present to our community at large significant voices articulating what I would term "true evangelical faith." The person heading this effort was Dr. Arthur Salibian, one of our outstanding plastic surgeons in Southern California and a keen mind in matters of theology and science. Subsequent to our coming together, he edited and then published an anthology of related articles in a book titled *Armenian Evangelicals' Challenge to Religious Extremism*, with the subtitle *The Growing Influence of Fundamentalism in Armenian Evangelical Churches* (published by ARMEVIEW, Arthur Salibian, Editor, 2015). I have written two chapters included in it: "What is an 'Evangelical'?" and "Use and Misuse of the Bible." In the course of these and other happenings, we have developed a close and strong friendship which brings us together from time to time to share views and discuss matters of mutual interest. In this, my wife, Samira, and Mrs. Nora Salibian share by joining us for social fellowship occasionally.

Presbyterians and the Armenian Genocide

April 24, 2015, was very significant for Armenians throughout the world. It was the one-hundredth anniversary of the Genocide which took the lives of 1.5 million of our people and eliminated them from their ancestral lands in eastern Turkey.

Several of us in the PC(USA) agreed to lend our efforts to have our national church, at its June 2014 General Assembly in Detroit, adopt a resolution (called an "overture") and go on record officially recognizing the Genocide. This effort was initiated by the leadership in the JMP (Jinishian Memorial Program, Eliza Minasyan, director and Cara Taylor, administrative assistant) which is a missions and humanitarian program for Armenians, affiliated with the PC(USA). It was written under the guidance of the Rev. Greg Allen-Picket, general manager, Presbyterian World Mission. For an overture to gain a hearing in a General Assembly, it must first be adopted by three local presbyteries, and then referred to G.A. for action. The three presbyteries that supported this overture were: Los Ranchos, Chicago, and Palisades (NJ). Here is the text:

In order to mark the Centennial of the Armenian genocide in 2015, to remember the suffering of the Armenian people, and to give thanks for their continuing witness, the Presbytery of Los Ranchos (with concurrence of the Presbytery of Chicago and the Presbytery of Palisades) respectfully overtures the 221st General Assembly of the Presbyterian Church (U.S.A) to take the following measures to testify to this tragedy and to help ensure that no other peoples experience such suffering:

1. Urge congregations and individuals to
    a. recognize the Armenian Genocide, which claimed 1.5 million lives of Armenians from 1915 to 1923 and displaced more than one million more;
    b. Express deep sympathy to the Armenian people and designate April 24th of every year hereafter a day of remembrance of the 1.5 million Armenians who fell victim to the first genocide of the twentieth century;
    c. Honor the provisions of American and international law and the role of American and international justice institutions in preventing the recurrence of similar mass killings, atrocities, and population removals and bringing the perpetrators of any such crimes to justice; and

Furthermore, believing that the international recognition of this genocide is a necessary condition for the prevention of similar crimes that may occur in the future, the General Assembly:

2. *Supports the designation of "genocide" for the deaths of 1.5 million Armenians and the expulsion of one million more from the Ottoman Empire during the period from 1915–1923, recognizing the systemic elimination of a population group as a crime against humanity in keeping with the 1947 Geneva Convention on Genocide,*

3. *Directs the Stated Clerk of the General Assembly to*

　　a. *Call upon President Obama and Congress of the United States of America to recognize and condemn the death and expulsion of Armenians from the Ottoman Empire as a genocide, and to communicate this resolution for that purpose:*

　　b. *Communicate this resolution to ecumenical partners and organizations nationally and internationally,*

　　c. *Ensure suitable time within the 222nd General Assembly (2016) to observe the anniversary of the Armenian Genocide and to honor those organizations, countries and individuals who assisted Armenian refugees, including the work of the Jinishian Memorial Program.*

4. *Directs the Presbyterian Mission Agency to*

　　a. *Encourage appropriate observance of the 100th anniversary of the Armenian Genocide, designating Sunday April 26, 2015, as the 100 year anniversary commemoration day in Presbyterian churches including the preparation of educational and liturgical resources, drawing on the witness of prior assemblies and other historical records, and participation in travel, conferences, and other memorials to be made available on the web at least two months prior to 4/26/2015;*

　　b. *Encourage the United States to endorse the highest human rights standards for all agencies and actions of the United States government, including protection of minority and/or subjugated populations from genocide and ethnic cleansing;*

c. Work cooperatively with other churches and communions in both advocacy and encouraging appropriate artistic, musical, and other cultural forms of remembrance.

Among the variety of resources prepared for churches to use in the annual commemoration of the Armenian Genocide on April 24, Dr. David Gambrell, associate for worship, Presbyterian Mission Agency, has written a beautiful congregational hymn titled, "Lord, to You Our People Cry." It was inspired by the opening and closing prayers of the *Book of Lamentations,* by Gregory of Narek (Grigor Narekatsi). It is reproduced in full (music and lyrics) in the Appendix.[4]

Bringing this matter to the floor of our presbytery (Los Ranchos) was easy, but having it heard and adopted for referral to the General Assembly was something else! As the person speaking in favor of this action, I was alone and vulnerable. To my great surprise and disappointment, a number of delegates, who had been my colleagues and friends, spoke in opposition to its adoption. However, with my deep gratitude, several of my friends spoke up in support of it. The arguments in opposition were essentially three:

1. "*It happened so long ago that it is history, and we should leave it there.*"

My response: If it is true that "justice delayed is justice denied" then the Armenians have had to live with justice denied for a long time. Atrocities and massacres have plagued the Armenians in Turkey periodically far much longer than one hundred years. However, in 1915 the systematic plan to get rid of them once for all was instituted, because Armenians have been a thorn in their side ever since they were invaded by Turkish hordes from central Asia over a thousand years ago. The 1915 Genocide was intentional extermination and ethnic cleansing.

2. "*We have Turkish friends who deny that it ever happened. They say that it was wartime and thousands died on both sides.*" (This is the official position taken by the Turkish government today)

---

4 See Appendix 3 for the full text.

My response: Most Turks have heard only their government's denialist responses to this question. One hears it all the time. However, when time and effort are put into searching for answers in terms of documents, determination by scholars, publications, eye-witness accounts, and official reports by British and American consular officials in Turkey, the truth emerges. The obvious result of one's search verifies that it was indeed genocide. Raphael Lemkin, the scholar and Holocaust survivor who invented the term "genocide," the definition of which was formally adopted in 1948 by the Geneva Convention on the Prevention and Punishment of the Crime of Genocide, publicly acknowledged (recorded in a CBS TV interview) that the term "genocide" fit the treatment of Armenians in the Ottoman Empire.

3. *"We are Christians. And we should follow the teaching of Jesus to love our enemies and forgive them."*

My response: Jesus taught us how to cope with hatred and violence so that the desire for revenge does not consume us. This we do, taking to heart Jesus's teaching, and we are able to live and function in relation to Turks today. However, forgiveness does not nullify the demand for recognition. To deny history is to deny our very selves and to live in a make-believe world.

It hurt me deeply to hear brothers in ministry, with whom I had served and labored for Christ, stand and oppose this resolution. It was a blow to my heart! During the debate I sat in complete isolation asking myself, "What will I do if the resolution does not pass?" I contemplated the possibility of walking out in protest. However, thank God it passed with a two to one plurality.

In June of 2014, I joined others on this mission of bringing the resolution to the General Assembly, which convened in Detroit, Michigan. Chicago Presbytery had sent the Rev. Dr. Christine Chakoian as their delegate. We two addressed the Peacemaking committee, which had to approve it before it could be sent to the floor of the plenary session for adoption. We were especially grateful for the added support and witness of one other speaker, the Rev. Fr. Garabed Kochakian, pastor of St. John

Armenian Apostolic Church of Detroit. We were overjoyed when the committee heard us and voted to accept the resolution. It was then sent on to the plenary session of the whole assembly on Friday, June 22. It was placed on the consent docket and eventually adopted with no dissenting voice.

I herein include my presentation before the Committee on June 16, for the sake of the record in my memoirs:

Friends, and colleagues in Christ. I come before you as a delegate from Los Ranchos Presbytery and a Presbyterian pastor for over 60 years. My first Presbyterian pastorate was in the First Armenian Presbyterian Church, Fresno, California, which was established in 1897. Yes, we've had an Armenian Presbyterian Church in America for over 100 years. I am a son of Armenian parents who somehow survived the terrible genocide years of 1915–1923. They witnessed much of what happened then, and passed on to us our heritage of Christian faith, and the tenacity which helped them and their children to survive and thrive. They ended up in Cyprus where they reestablished their lives.

Most importantly, I stand before you in memory and honor of a million and a half Armenians who perished, and whose existence and future in their ancestral homelands in eastern Anatolia, Turkey, were wiped out. Hence, we use the term genocide. These were lands where they existed from ancient times. However, from times dating back to the Persian Empire, they have suffered persecutions because of their Christian faith.

I also rise to appeal to you, and our General Assembly, to adopt this Overture, pointing us to the year 2015, when we will observe the 100th Anniversary. By doing so we encourage the international recognition of this genocide as an important witness for the prevention of similar genocides anywhere in our world today. Our Presbyterian Church is not ignorant of the facts and events relative to this matter. Dispatches, eye-witness accounts from missionaries in the field there, and resolutions by early General Assemblies on this issue, (such as in 1918, 1919, 1920), are plentiful and a matter of public record. Added to their reports are those of many others, including officials of governments who were witnesses to the atrocities, massacres, and forced deportations of our people. Among these are the notable Viscount Bryce of Great Britain in his volume of accumulated reports submitted to the British government. We also have the witness of the American Ambassador to Turkey at that time, Henry Morgenthau, who has it clearly documented in his book, "The Murder of a Nation."

We consider it very important that the term Genocide be used in reference to this subject, because it fits the definition of the term, as coined by Raphael Lemkin in 1943, and adopted in 1948 by the United Nations Convention on the Prevention and Punishment of Genocide. He personally acknowledged this to be a fact, when in a CBS video interview he said, "I became interested in genocide because it happened many times. It happened to the Armenians, and after the Armenians Hitler took action." Thus it must be noted that the precursor to the Holocaust of the Jews in Europe was the Armenian Genocide. Germany was aligned with Ottoman Turkey, during World War I, and provided logistical and military support. The plan for the extermination of Armenians was executed with their knowledge. Years later Hitler followed the same diabolical plan in regards to the Jews in Europe.

Thus the first genocide of the 20th Century was put into effect. These atrocities were not the result of the revolt of the Armenians in a civil war, but the plan to eliminate Armenians in Turkey. It started on April 24, 1915, with the public hanging of 200 leaders in Istanbul. Then, in coordinated action, men were rounded up in towns and villages, and led to their execution. Old men, women and children remaining behind were forced out of their homes and marched miles away to their destination in the deserts of Syria, where they were abandoned to starvation and death. The remnants, who survived, were rescued and cared for by the Middle East Relief programs in which American churches and civic organizations, such as the Red Cross, participated. In Syria, this remnant worked to develop their lives. Schools, churches, orphanages and hospitals were established. Alas, today they are in ruins again, and thousands are flee-ing to safer havens.

Let me stress that it is not revenge but recognition and remembrance that we seek. This deep wound in our hearts and our collective psyche can-not be healed unless our church, and our world beyond the Armenians, not only hear our story but respond with a resounding "Yes!" to our ap-peal. Thank you for your attention and action in our behalf.

As a pastor, I've had to deal with this issue from the very beginning of my ministry. The question of "Where was God during those years of terror, forced marches into the deserts, death of our people, and their abandonment?" continues to haunt us. This question is asked within the context of the larger question regarding suffering and God's will. I have heard it countless times, "Where is God? Why is God silent?" Shortly after we had moved from New York to Fresno, sometime around 1972, I called on my father to see how he was doing. An Armenian man from the neighborhood was visiting him. My dad proudly introduced me to him with the words, "Meet Rev. Vartkes, my son." After greeting me in return, he looked me straight in the eyes and asked, "So you are a pastor. Do you believe in God?"

"I most certainly do," I answered.

"I do not have a God. My God died in 1915," he sadly replied. Of course he was referring to the genocide of 1915.

I have never forgotten that incident, and it often comes back to haunt me. I admired my parents immensely on this issue. Both my father and my mother went through those terrible times, and I know they had personal encounters with Turks. My mother's first fiancé was murdered in plain view in Marash. My father, as a young man in Aintab (now called Gaziantep), was proud of his heritage, and at times came to the aid of his people who were being set upon in the streets. However, I've never heard him talk derisively about Turks, and I've never heard him doubt his faith in God. How could these two men become so far apart in their relationship and belief about God? My father reminds me of Job who in the midst of his misery said, "Though he (God) slay me, yet will I trust in him." (KJ Version) His belief and faith system went far beyond the question of whether God did really exist but to the point where his faith was centered in Jesus Christ as his Lord and Savior. He studied the Bible regularly and taught Bible classes in our church and in our school. I wish he were here today so I could ask him, "Dad, how did you do it? Why is God not dead for you?" I would then thank him and mom for raising us up with love, and for passing on to us their story, and the story of our people, without a call for vengeance. They freed us up to be people without the deep seething anger and bitterness that many sustain to this day.

In my lifelong search for an answer to this and accompanying questions about the presence and response of God to the suffering of innocent people, I have come to center my attention more and more on the meaning of Christ's suffering and death. The line in the Apostle's Creed that speaks to me and our human condition of undeserved suffering and death, is the line that says, he "was crucified, (was)dead and (was) buried; he descended into hell." On the cross when he cried out, "My God, my God, why have you forsaken me?" he experienced the terrible alienation and separation from God that our people, and all innocent people, experience in their suffering and destruction. Christ's descent into "hell" tells me God is there when we also find ourselves in the depth of hell on this earth. I know in our churches today we do not say "he descended into hell," but "he descended to the dead" to soften the sound of the word "hell" on our ears. In Holy Week, we jump from Good Friday (his crucifixion) to Easter (his resurrection). How about Holy Saturday? That's the day of his descent into hell! Exactly! And that's where God finds us and raises us up with the risen Christ! Faith does not abandon us there. Unfortunately, many people who give up on God, like my father's neighbor, do not have an escape from their torment. Where we find God in our suffering is right with us, suffering with us. God has not abandoned our people. God is with us still!

A Resolute Man and His Legacy

There have been a significant number of philanthropists who have devoted their life's mission to the service of the Armenian people. Working mostly through the many educational, ecclesiastical, and social programs of the Armenian Missionary Association of America, their legacy has been documented and publicly acknowledged. I cannot possibly do justice to them all, were I to start naming them herein. However, one man stands out in my experience, who has gone incognito for many years, and whose story needs to be told. He is Mr. Vartan Jinishian.

In America, very few people have ever heard of Vartan H. Jinishian, but it is different in Armenia and the Middle East. There he is well known and admired. His legacy is not remembered by statues or monuments erected in his honor, but in the lives of thousands of Armenians who were in need of humanitarian aid and who have received it and prospered because of it. Starting with the survivors of the Armenian genocide and continuing today with thousands of our people who are again displaced and in abject need, that legacy continues to grow in dimension and impact.

It began with a $10,000,000 endowment fund established in 1966 in memory of his parents, the Rev. Haroutune and Catherine Jinishian of Marash, Turkey, under the auspices of the Presbyterian Church (USA). For a number of years before that, Mr. Jinishian provided significant support in Syria and Lebanon for suffering Armenians but chose to remain incognito. He was the "Anonymous Donor" giving through the Howard Karagheusian Commemorative Corporation. He maintained his anonymity through it all, and never visited the countries where these services were being provided.

Vartan Jinishian was born in 1870 in Marash but moved to New York City when he was eighteen years old. He eventually ended up working for H. and M. Karagheusian, Inc., which pioneered in the machine production of oriental design rugs and other carpeting. He eventually climbed up the corporate ladder to the position of partner. He was a confirmed bachelor, living frugally and maintaining the values of hard work, faith, and spirituality, instilled in him by his parents. He was an expert antique rug collector and dealer traveling in Europe and up and down the East Coast for his business, including the White House in Washington, DC. He had an apartment in Paris where he kept and traded his collection of antique rugs and furniture. He is reputed to have said, "If a rug is worth less than $50,000, I'm not interested." He also invested in real estate, eventually amassing a fortune. In Manhattan he owned prime properties on Madison Avenue, and also on Fifty-Seventh Street.

He was a quiet and unassuming person. He was leery of people who kept trying to see him to solicit contributions to charitable causes. His secretary was instructed to keep solicitors waiting and waiting, until they gave up and left. Even though he amassed a fortune and was very wealthy, he did not care to spend much on himself, beyond maintaining a simple and comfortable life. He retired in the 1940s, but he kept an office at the Karagheusian firm in Mid-Manhattan.

He was a member of the Armenian Evangelical community of New York but attended from time to time the Fifth Avenue and Madison Avenue Presbyterian churches. I got to know him when I pastored the Armenian Evangelical Church of New York City in the early 1960s. Once, in 1960, I visited him in his office to discuss with him a ninetieth birthday gathering we planned for him, at the residence of his friends, Mr. and Mrs. D. H. Armaghanian of Forest Hills. His office was simple and looked like nothing had changed since its early years. He did agree to come to the gathering in his honor but insisted it be kept very simple. I thought presenting him with a new pen and pencil desk set, mounted on an onyx base, would enhance the decor of his office. Upon presenting this gift to him during the birthday party, he looked rather puzzled and said, "I don't need this. I already have pens and pencils. Take it back!"

The commonly held impression of Vartan Jinishian, the man, was one of a secluded and self-absorbed person who was very rich but kept it all to himself, like a miser. This image of him began to change quickly and dramatically when knowledge of his philanthropic nature began to emerge, mostly after his death. It became known that the mysterious "anonymous donor" who had been supporting poor families and their children in Syria, Lebanon, and other localities in the Middle East, with day nurseries, lunch programs, and other social services was none other than Mr. Jinishian. He carried on these humanitarian works by way of the Karagheusian Corporation. He not only maintained a low profile through it all but also quietly worked on a plan to develop his legacy.

The key person who helped Mr. Jinishian in this regard was Mr. Edward Janjigian. Sometime in the late 1950s he was introduced to Mr. Jinishian as a business man who traveled often between New York and the Middle East. He offered to help Mr. Jinishian by bringing him information about the projects funded there by him. When Mr. Jinishian was made aware that this service was being offered at no cost, he agreed. Mr. Janjigian made as many as three trips a year to the project sites and made his reports in person upon his return. He was well-known to the Armenian Evangelical community in New York and New Jersey. He and his wife, Lucy, were members of our church in New York City, until they moved to New Jersey and transferred their membership to a Presbyterian church there. They were active in the Armenian Missionary Association as key leaders as well. With his encouragement, Mr. Jinishian agreed to move and take up residence in a retirement home in Pleasanton, New Jersey, with care oversight provided by the Presbyterian church.

At that time formal negotiations with the United Presbyterian Church in the United States. via its foreign missions division called COEMAR (Commission On Ecumenical Mission And Relations) were carried on until they all eventually agreed to receive and establish his estate in the form of an endowment "Fund in memory of Rev. Haroutune and Catherine Jinishian of Marash, Turkey." Being unhappy with the rivalries and tension existing between Armenian denominations and organizations, he found in the United Presbyterian Church a neutral and trusted body to administer his endowment fund. Before his death in 1966, plans were finalized, and as mandated by his will, they were put into effect. The fund would be held in perpetuity by the United Presbyterian Church in America (The precursor to the Presbyterian Church USA) and administered by a committee including Protestant, Roman Catholic, and Armenian Apostolic representatives. The income generated by this fund would only be used to provide the services for the needy and the underprivileged so dear to his heart. Thus the Jinishian Memorial Fund has been at work bringing sorely needed aid to our people.

Celebrating Retirement

Family gathered to celebrate my retirement at a special luncheon
(missing, Timothy and family). Tustin Presbyterian Church, December 28, 2014.

Armenian Advocacy

Strategizing with Carl Horton, Mission Coordinator for the Peacemaking Committee, prior to the historic vote on the overture regarding the Armenian Genocide at the PC(USA) General Assembly. Detroit, Michigan, June 2014.

Delegates in plenary session at the historic General Assembly.

The vote was unanimous to recommend adoption of the overture to the General Assembly Plenary Session.

(Center) The Rev. Dr. Chris Chakoian and *(left)* Ms. Cara Taylor (Jinishian Memorial Program) worked hard in formulating the overture and following its path to success.

Ten

Going to Armenia has its rewards, however going there with a mission has special and unexpected rewards. Samira and I had the privilege of going there in June of 2015 and connecting with the programs of Jinishian Foundation and the Armenian Missionary Association of America (AMAA). After first meeting Mr. Jinishian over fifty years ago, I now had the privilege of observing the realization of his vision over fifty years later. My initial association with the AMAA was in 1953 when as a seminary student I used to walk from our school on Forty-Ninth Street down to Thirty-Third Street in New York City (their old location before they moved to Paramus, New Jersey). I offered them my services as a volunteer. The director was the Rev. Puzant Kalfayan, whom I admired as a gifted man of God. He eventually asked me if I'd be interested to come on as his assistant after I graduated. I was positively inclined to do so, but alas, he died of a heart attack, and his career as a great leader of our people ended prematurely.

In America we first connected with the Jinishian Program when their Director, Eliza Minasyan, came to California in 2012. I introduced her and the program to a number of our community leaders. Since then we have been their enthusiastic supporters. So it was that Samira and I traveled to Armenia and witnessed in person a variety of their ministries. This mission was instrumental in creating and maintaining a number of self-help projects in a variety of locations in Armenia. I had always wanted to return to Armenia, after my first short trip there in 1969, but I waited for the right time and set of circumstances to make it possible. Adding to this unique experience was the fact that my grandson, Spencer May, was at that time in Yerevan as a volunteer with Birthright Armenia, teaching science in a prestigious high school. He was learning Armenian and loving every day there. His mother, my daughter Karen, his father Dr. Pete May, his brother Lucas, and his sister Aubrey, were also all there at that time. So we had a grand and totally serendipitous reunion. As they say, "it was a blast!"

The executive director of JMP (Jinishian Memorial Program) in Armenia was Mr. Armen Hakobyan. He and Eliza Minasyan were the brain and heart of this whole enterprise, along with their dedicated staff of about half a dozen men and women. It was obvious to us that theirs was not a job but a mission to which they all were totally dedicated. Whether Armen or Eliza personally drove us, or one of their staff did, we covered city and country, mountain and valley, village and farm, church and cathedral, schools and hospitals, adults and children, farmers and workers, priests and villagers. We broke bread with the people in their homes. We ate delicious ripe apricots (this country is where they originated) and cherries sold along the way, right next to the trees loaded with fruit. We drank from the ice-cold waters flowing in mountain brooks and savored their delicious breads served to us right out of the baker's ovens.

Here is an example of their hospitality. One of our visits was in the village of Odzun with its historic church edifice, dating to the twelfth century AD. We were guests of Fr. Vrtanes Baghalian and family. When we walked up to the house, we smelled lamb roasting on an open fire. Father Vrtanes, with shirtsleeves rolled up, was at the fire barbequing our lunch. With open arms he welcomed us and proudly introduced his family to us. He then showed us his beehives and his fruit trees. It was his daughter's birthday, and we joined in singing a hearty "Happy Birthday" together. Then we sat around the table to enjoy the delicious meal prepared by *yeretsgin* (meaning the priest's wife) and him. Following that, he put on his clerical robe and led us on a tour of the church. With great pride he showed us just about every stone, each of which had a historical significance. We will always remember the village of Odzun and Fr. Vrtanes.

We were awe struck by history and story, told by silent churches and thousands of *khatchkars* (cross-stones), standing in eloquent silence and speaking to us in hushed tones only a heart could hear. These intricately carved stones, with a cross in the center surrounded by fruits, flowers, and geometric patterns delicately carved like lace-work, are unique to the landscape in Armenia. They were used as headstones in cemeteries and as sentinels in and around churches. Adding to their impact were the ancient paintings and manuscripts of the Holy Bible in the Museum (*Madenadaran*) and Cathedral (*Etchmiadzin*). This is where the Catholicos abides and is the very obvious center of the country's identity and life.

This story is still being written today, in blood, sweat, and tears, as eloquently recounted by our guide in Stepanakert, the capital of Nagorno-Karabagh (Karabagh or Artsakh, as known by the people). He was a veteran of the war for the independence of that region of ancient Armenia, which was arbitrarily ceded to Azerbaijan by the USSR (Joseph Stalin) in 1923, even though over 90 percent of the citizens were Armenian. In 1994, after the breakup of the Soviet Union, it was reclaimed by Armenians in a three-year war that took the lives of several thousand. Azerbaijan has not given up their claim to the land, and from time to time fighting breaks out on the borders. However, these hardy people swear they will never give up their land again. Talks continue among the parties involved, and their longing for peace remains a matter of constant vigilance and prayer.

I have two distinct impressions relative to the dedication and effectiveness of the Jinishian Program in Armenia. First, the lack of ostentation. There are no lush quarters and offices, but in simplicity all resources are dedicated to their mission. For example, we walked up five flights of stairs in a building built in the Stalin era, with no elevator, to reach the offices of the organization.

Second, the way in which they connect with the people of the land. There is no "charity" there but support for projects which the people themselves determine are to be their priorities. Whether on a farm or in a village, they organize for action accordingly. It is then that JMP offers support. We met with farmers overjoyed that they had received necessary support to build a small concrete dam to hold waters of a stream supplying sorely needed water for irrigation.

I met with a group of young college graduates in the village of Vardenis who had banded together for community development. Their purpose was to provide support for achieving human rights, economic justice, and environmental health. They bragged that they had the cleanest village in the area because of the success of their efforts. They were not alone in this. Five groups from other regions joined them several days later in Aghveran for the annual conference of Youth in Action for Change, to compare notes, share their experiences, and strategize for their future. I watched, listened, and took photos of these smart and highly motivated young people working to carry on their program. It was very inspiring to behold. God bless them!

The Jinishian Program is nonsectarian and nonreligious in accordance with the express wishes of the benefactor. However, also in accordance with the benefactor's plan, it has a board with representation of the three major religious groups in Armenia, Lebanon/Syria, and the United States: Roman Catholic, Armenian Apostolic, and Evangelical (Protestant). They do not only participate in its administration but also receive financial support to add finances needed beyond what Jinishian Fund provides. Their objective is not religious but humanitarian, pure and simple.

Connecting with the AMAA in Armenia

For over sixty years I have been aware of and involved in another organization dedicated to the spiritual, educational, and physical welfare of the

Armenian people worldwide. To initially address the plight of the post-genocide remnant of the Armenian people, the Armenian Missionary Association of America (AMAA) was organized by dedicated and visionary people in the United States in 1918, with the support of our churches both on the East Coast and on the West Coast.

The AMAA has grown significantly, in terms of financial resources, and is actively involved in providing support and aid in a number of Middle Eastern countries and in America as well. They have been doing a fantastic job of standing with our people everywhere with compassion and love. We thank God for visionary people like Stephen Philibosian, Mr. and Mrs. Steve Mehagian, Judge Nazareth Barsumian, Hekemian family, Sheen Family, and many others, who dedicated themselves and their resources to this worthy cause. Their legacy is carried forward with vision and enthusiasm by members of their families, such as Joyce (Philibosian) and Joe Stein.[5]

As a pastor and spiritual leader in our churches, I have worked beyond being a cheer-leader to rallying our people to support it. In the 1960s and 1970s when I was the moderator of the Armenian Evangelical Union on several occasions, I had two serious concerns which I shared with their executive director, Dr. Giragos Chopourian and also with the board of directors on a number of occasions. The first dealt with the question of the difference between the AMAA and the AEU (Armenian Evangelical Union). My point was, and continues to be, that the AMAA is a mission organization, while the AEU is an ecclesiastical one. The AMAA must defer to the Union when it comes to such matters as ordination of clergy, establishment of new churches, and oversight over them. The AEU had no fund-raising efforts except in support of the AMAA.

This matter became critical when the AEU decided to support our Canadian brethren in Toronto with buying a building. (I have alluded to this earlier.) Leaders in the AMAA refused to support this project, hence the AEU had to do its own fund-raising. Beginning with this project the

---

5 The full story of the AMAA can be received by applying directly to them: info@amaa.org, or writing to AMAA 31 West Century Rd., Paramus, NJ 07652, USA.

AMAA and AEU have now developed a cooperative effort where needed funds are provided.

The other matter is that of the function of the AEU as an ecclesiastical overseer in matters of the education and then the ordination of clergy. The AMAA should not act in this capacity because it is not an ecclesiastical body but the mission agency of the churches that have created and sustained it. I have wondered how this matter is worked out in Armenia, because according to my understanding, it is the AMAA that is in charge in all these matters there. In Lebanon and Syria there is a strong cooperative relationship which is positive and healthy.

As a result of my openly asking these questions, and sharing my concerns, I became a "burr under the saddles" of my dear friends in the AMAA, and I was kept at arms length for a long time. I loved Dr. Chopourian since my boyhood days. He was my Sunday school teacher and my teacher also in the American Academy. He was also my Boy Scout leader and my field hockey coach. After we both left Cyprus we lost track of each other, until we both came together again in our church-related life and community in America. After we both attained leadership roles (he in the AMAA and I in the AEU), when it came to these issues, we often did not see eye to eye.

We love the AMAA and are deeply committed to it. We have continually supported it for years, and I have served on their board of directors as well. Their outreach ministries, educational and social service projects can be found in all the countries of the Middle East, and several other countries. I have observed a number of them throughout the years. While in Armenia, although my time and focus was the Jinishian Memorial Program, I made it a point to also connect with the AMAA representatives and the Armenian Evangelical churches with the limited time I had. Mr. Harout Nercessian, the director of the program, graciously welcomed us and offered to lead us for visits to their schools, centers, and ministry locations. Their headquarters are located in Yerevan, on Bagramian Street, in the former American Embassy building.

Behind this structure is the Armenian Evangelical Church of Yerevan. We attended worship service there one Sunday and participated in the fellowship time afterward. The pastor there is the Rev. Mgrdich Melkonian, who was formerly the pastor of First Armenian Presbyterian Church in Fresno for several years before he accepted a call to come to Armenia. He is the pastor to pastors for all the spiritual leaders and pastors there. However, the Sunday we attended he was away, and the associate pastor, the Rev. Hovhannes Hovsepian was the worship leader. He was eloquent in preaching and very warm in extending their welcome to us. Attendance was around 150 people, with whom we mingled during the fellowship time. It is noteworthy that their style of service was quite contemporary, copying the style popular in America today.

When we were in Vardenis (on the southeastern shore of Lake Sevan), I visited with Mr. Armen Movsisyan, the spiritual head of a small Evangelical church there. With the help of the AMAA, a commercial building was bought and converted into a worship center, seating around fifty people. He drove me to their home where I met Mrs. Movsisyan and their children. We enjoyed a cup of Armenian coffee and chatted for a while. In the course of our conversation, I found out that he is still a student of theology and not yet ordained. I shared with him my admiration for him and his family for carrying on their witness to Christ in that location and assured him of our continuing interest and prayers.

Of special note was our visit to the Avedisian Education Center in Yerevan, whose benefactors are Edward and Pamela Avedisian of Boston, Massachusetts. The center is named after his parents, Khoren and Shooshanig Avedisian. We had been hearing about this new and modern institution for the past several years, and that it would be costing around $15 million. Well, we were not disappointed. More than a school, it is a showcase of the most up-to-date architectural and technical achievements. It makes use of solar energy and other innovations, placing this institution in the forefront of Armenia's recent achievements. It was the first to be built with LEEDS certification (Leadership in Energy and Environmental Design). In the auditorium, we were delighted to hear and be entertained by the children rehearsing their songs for an upcoming festival. It was a fitting climax to a special visit indeed.

That same evening, Karen's family joined Samira and me for a great dinner at the Aintab Restaurant near our hotel (Aintab, now called Gaziantep, is where my father came from in Turkey). While we enjoyed our meal I noticed a couple seated at a table close to ours. The gentleman kept glancing at me, and I kept eyeing him, thinking that he looked somewhat familiar. Well, I finally went to their table and introduced myself. To my great surprise they were Edward and Pamela Avedisian in person. He said that he, too, kept thinking I looked familiar, wondering who I was. We had never met in person before but had seen photos of each other in AMAA publications. We shared with them our joy in visiting the school and our thanks for their philanthropy in support of our people.

The American University of Armenia in Yerevan had a special interest for me. It is a great project and undertaking of the Armenian General Benevolent Union (AGBU), and its founding president was Dr. Mihran Agbabian, whom we've known for many years. It is a magnificent institution which started with some two hundred students, twenty-five years ago, and today it has more than two thousand. It was established by the Armenian General Benevolent Union (AGBU) in 1991, the year of Armenia's independence. We had a visit with the president of AUA, Dr. Armen Der Kiureghian, who shared with us the growing size and reach and influence of the school. He is also a renowned artist whose paintings were on display in a gallery on the premises there. It was especially significant for me to know that Eliza Minasyan, director of the Jinishian Program, was one of their early graduates. She affirmed what has been a unique feature of the university: in a typical class session, the students are invited and encouraged to ask questions, to present their points of view, and to agree or disagree with the professor's or others' viewpoints. "This is unique for Armenia," she stressed, "and that is why I value so very much the education I received at AUA."

Upon entering their main building, we were ushered to the hall, where in prominent display was a portrait of Dr. Mihran Agbabian, the founding president of the university, which he served for six years, and his wife Elizabeth, daughter of the much-loved and respected Rev. Hovhannes and Aznive Apkarian. This amazing couple has been at the forefront of Armenian humanitarian causes for years.

I digress intentionally to pay tribute to them and their devotion. Brothers Mihran and Hrant and their sister Lucina (who went to be with the Lord in 2015) have made their mark of distinction in many ways. Mihran headed the Agbabian, Jacobson and Associates civil engineering firm, and subsequent to that he became the head of the Department of Civil and Environmental Engineering at the University of Southern California. Hrant is a renowned architect (AIA Architects and Associates), musician, and sculptor. He directed for many years the one-hundred-member choral group, which he organized, called Pro Gomidas Choral Society. For many years he was the choir director of United Armenian Congregational Church of Los Angeles. Their sister, Lucina, was a distinguished soprano, whose lovely voice was heard all over Southern California. She also excelled in researching and teaching, in private groups and at USC, the treasures of Armenian music.

The Kassouni family in Cyprus had the privilege of having their parents, the Rev. Siragan and Parouhi Agbabian, as their pastoral team in the early 1930s. Rev. Siragan wrote the preface, titled "Two Words," to introduce a volume of Psalms put to music for congregational singing in Armenian, a book authored by my father, and his brother, the Rev. Yeghia Kassouny. It is dated May 23, 1931 (the year I was born). When Mihran was on his way to America in 1946, he made a stop in Larnaca to bid farewell and to receive the blessings of his friends. For the occasion, my mother arranged a reception for him in our home. I remember it well because it was my duty to roast the chestnuts on a stove and serve them hot to our guests.

After one week's time in Armenia, Samira had to fly back to the United States to carry on her teaching schedule. From then on I continued the journey of discovery and education on my own.

Two other AMAA-related projects were my desire to observe while still in Armenia. One, their Sheen Camp in Hankavan. This I was able to do, but unfortunately only workers were on site, and preparations were being made for the camping programs to begin a month later. This camp was being renovated with several impressive buildings and beautiful grounds. That complex used to be a resort for workers in the Soviet era. It is now a year-round facility to accommodate youth and adults alike for camps and conferences. Harout Nercession (director of AMAA, Armenia) was there as my guide and host, and subsequent to that we spent time together to discuss relevant issues of mission and theology.

The other project that I was hoping to visit was the AMAA Camp Bedrosian in Shushi, Nagorno Karabagh (also known by the locals as *Artsakh*). This was a summer camp which the Bedrosian family in Fowler, California, had sponsored. It is still a mission priority for them, and Bryan Bedrosian, son of Ernest and Carlotta Bedrosian, travels there quite often to maintain a hands-on involvement. Unfortunately, my short trip to Karabagh of only one day prevented me from actually going there. It remains on my to-do list when I travel there again.

My one day in Stepanagert, the capital, was when I finally connected with my second cousin, Vrej Kassouny. I had been wanting to see him but kept missing him in Armenia. He is a renowned political and social cartoonist whose incisive commentary on current events are prized throughout the land. He is also the person who organizes and directs the annual ReAnimania International Animation and Film Festival, bringing people in that field of art to Armenia from around the world. We had dinner together in an Italian-style restaurant on the public square, with significant civic and public buildings highlighted by floodlight. We had much to talk about relating to our families and our common interests. He was there for the filming of a movie about Karabagh in which he had a leading role.

During the day I was driven all over the country, my guide being a man who was a veteran of the 1991–94 war for independence from Azerbaijan, as written in earlier pages. He recounted story after story of their struggle and eventual success. The most intriguing one was the story of how the war finally came to an end with a truce arranged by Russia. It involved the saga of Shushi, a town on the brow of a high cliff overlooking Stepanagert, the capital, in the valley below. The Azeris had control of that high ground and kept up a barrage of fire pinning down the Armenians in the city below. It took the daring exploit of a number of volunteers to break that siege. Secretly, and quietly, they scaled those cliffs at night and surprised the enemy from the rear, which had been left relatively unprotected. Thus, when the Azeris realized that they were outflanked and could no longer protect the town of Shushi, fighting stopped. Under the provisions of a truce, negotiated by Russia, several thousand Azeri soldiers were given safe passage, and the war ended. The truce has been in effect for over twenty years, but there is the constant fear that war will resume. In April of 2016, fighting did break out, and scores of soldiers and civilians gave their life to repel the invading Azeris. Intermittent talks for a peace treaty continue to take place, with the key party, Russia, playing the risky role of go-between.

The Jinishian Program

The dedicated team of Jinishian Program office personnel,
led by Armen Hakobyan, Armenia,
and Eliza Minassyan, International Director *(second from the right)*.

(Inset) Mr. Vartan Jinishian, benefactor, in whose honor the program is named.

A typical community project in Armenia, funded by the Jinishian Program.

Beautiful Armenia

Mount Ararat, historic symbol for Armenia,
with the famous Monastery of Khor Virab in the foreground,
where Gregory the Illuminator, father of Christian Armenia, was held in prison.

At a historic ancient Armenian church edifice on the shores of Lake Sevan.

With Father Barouyr, a member of the Jinishian Advisory Board in Armenia,
in the museum of the Etchmiadzin Cathedral.

Ancient church at the village of Odzun, Armenia. Fr. Vrtanes, local priest.

Ancient church at Noravank, Armenia.

Ghazanchetsots Cathedral at Shushi, Nagorno-Karabakh.

Eleven

What Now?

In January 2015, I ended all formal relations with Tustin Presbyterian Church and retired. "What, again?" was the response, in jest, of many to my announcement. This decision freed me up and gave me time to pursue other interests. The most challenging was an invitation in March of 2014 from Carl Horton, in charge of the Peacemaking Program, PC(USA), to join the International Peacemaker program in the fall of 2014. They asked me to speak in several churches in the Northwest, with a focus on the Middle East and Armenia. This I did, going in October first to Juneau, Alaska, and then to Bellingham, Washington. Since I had recently spent three weeks in Armenia, I was equipped with many photos and stories to share, calling their attention to the history of Armenians and their Genocide of 1915–23 in Ottoman Turkey.

In March 2015, I was invited to be a global leader in residence at Westminster College, Fulton, Missouri. It was one intense, challenging, and rewarding week spent among students and faculty of this small and prestigious Presbyterian-related college. This is the college where Winston Churchill spoke on March 5, 1946, at the invitation of President Harry Truman. There is a commanding statue of Churchill on the college grounds, next to their chapel, recalling the historic day on March 5, 1946, when in his famous speech he used the term, "Iron curtain," describing the beginning of the Cold War with the Soviet Union. At the base of the statue is a quote from that speech, "An iron curtain has descended across the continent." Since then, the term Iron Curtain has been used to signify the separation of the Western world from Eastern Europe and the Soviet Union, until the demise of the USSR in 1989. A section of the actual Berlin Wall has been moved and placed on the campus common. While there I stayed in a Victorian-style bed and breakfast hotel, made famous by Margaret Thatcher, former prime minister of England, who was their guest when she visited the college. Addressing several classes and having small group gatherings with the students was the highlight of this trip. The subjects were varied, from the meaning of spirituality, to the Armenian Genocide of 1915–23, and the current events and wars being waged in the Middle East. I love the intellectual and spiritual ferment so easily evident among college students. Too bad I limited my life work to the local church scene. I should have gotten involved much earlier with the college scene as well.

Tears of Sorrow, Tears of Joy

Retirement has opened up for me a fine mix and variety of activities and experiences. At the top of my list is family interests. In May of 2015, I traveled to Cyprus on the occasion of the passing of my elder sister, Nouvart, at the age of ninety-two years. She was a most unusual and talented person, acknowledged and respected throughout the island. She was a school teacher at the American Academy for girls, in Nicosia. She was a mezzo soprano, singing in concerts and on radio. She had formed a choir of talented singers, whose concerts are still remembered as being exceptional. She and her husband, Hercules, started a community church in Nicosia, which continues to this day.

Olivette, my brother Sarkis's wife, passed away in May of this year, 2016. My brother Sarkis had passed away in 2000. I went to Grand Rapids,

Michigan, on June 27 for a service celebrating her life. We gathered in the social hall of the Episcopal Church in Greenville, where she was a member. Sarkis predeceased her fifteen years ago. The saying "still waters run deep" describes Olivette. She was strong of will and had a sharp intellect. She raised her four sons and deserves a medal for it, because each is unique, independent, with creative talents in business and private life.

My nephew, Ted (Nouvart's son), had come from Sudbury, Canada for the occasion. The day after our gathering, we took off on a four-day trip south, taking us through Pennsylvania, Washington DC and back. First, we stopped overnight at the home of his cousin, Allen and Larissa Mavrides in Munroe Falls, Ohio (near Kent). Allen's father was my teacher in the American Academy. We had a lovely time there, including a couple of sets of tennis, with Allen and his granddaughter Lexi, playing against Ted and me. They are excellent players, but we held our own just fine.

We continued our journey from there with the plan to stop in three places: West Pittston, Pennsylvania; Willow Street, Pennsylvania (near Lancaster); and Washington, DC. My main objective was to visit with my sister, Agnes, and her husband Dr. Richard Scribner, in Willow Street, whom I had not seen for several years. We also intended to visit with Ted's Aunt Phoula in Washington, DC. In America it is so easy to lose close contact with family and friends due to the separation of time and of geography. Making special effort to do so, however, has its rewards. In my later years I have become quite conscious of this and confess that I have not maintained the ties that I should have done. Social media, such as Facebook, of which I am a member, and which seems to be the overwhelming trend, is not much help either. All of society is caught up in this wave, like a tsunami, but nothing can take the place of person-to-person, face-to-face visits to maintain warmth and intimacy of human relationships. Hence we took this trip to the East to see friends and relatives. The problem with doing this, however, is that each visit brings up other names of people which we should also visit, but alas, the restraint of time and resources prevent us from doing so. Consequently the feelings of guilt, in this regard, continue largely unabated.

On our way there, we stopped for a visit with the Rev. Dr. John and Inge Markarian, in West Pittston, Pennsylvania (near Scranton). They lived in his parent's house, an old, beautiful, and gracious home of historic designation, right on the southern bank of the Susquehanna River. John and I have known each other since the early 1950s. He was a professor at Lafayette College, in upstate New York, when he was chosen by the Board of AMAA to be the first president of Haigazian College, in Beirut. When I was in seminary, he tried hard to get me to go to Haigazian and teach there also, but it never worked out so that I could. He served this newly established institution with distinction, solidifying the school's internal strength, and growth. He and Inga were there through the thick and thin of the Civil War that engulfed Lebanon from the 1970s, to the late 1980s. His story of those terrible years is told in his memoir titled *The Thirsty Enemy* (AMAA publication, 2009, amaa@amaa.org). They lived in Los Angeles for several years after their return from Beirut. He and I used to play tennis together on the courts of the Ambassador Hotel, where Robert Kennedy was assassinated in 1968. Alas, that grand historic hotel is no more, having fallen victim to the developers' wrecking ball.

John is a unique person with a keen mind, astute theological insight, and a sense of humor that has served him well over the years. His wife, Inge, is a very special person in her own right. She is a lovely and gracious lady and very talented as an artist; her paintings are special indeed, with some hanging on the walls of their house. She is also a collector of antique Middle Eastern artifacts and jewelry, and creates new jewelry, using her finds.

Our very memorable visit with them had to be hurried because we had to get to our next destination with my sister. We made it in time to have dinner with Richard and their son Daniel. We then proceeded to visit with Agnes. She has been quite incapacitated with Parkinson's and was limited to a wheel chair. What a change for somebody who was always active, and used to play tennis every day in Wilmington, where they lived until retirement. We used to play tennis together in Cyprus before we both came to the United States. Back problems hounded her with no help coming from surgeries. She then developed Parkinson's and now is confined to her room mostly.

From Willow Street we drove to Washington DC, to visit with Ted's Aunt Phoula, who turned ninety the past year. My sister Nouvart and Phoula were very close friends. Her husband, Hercules, was Phoula's brother. In Cyprus, where we all resided, our families were in the same community/village that raised us. Phoula was in a physical rehab hospital following surgery and doing quite well. We stayed with Ariadne, her daughter, whom I had never met before. She is a sharp realtor and a charming person. This short, and yet lovely, visit with her and her mother was a treat indeed.

While we were in Washington, DC, Ted and I visited with the Ambassador from Cyprus to the United States, the Honorable Mr. Leonidas Pantelides. Ted and he had been schoolmates in the English School, in Nicosia, and that provided a great entree for us. In the course of our visit, we discussed the ever-present topic of the division of Cyprus between the Turkish and Greek sides and the prospect of resolving the matter and realizing unity again. The island was invaded by Turkey in 1974, using the excuse that the Turkish minority needed to be protected in the turbulent political times when Greek nationalists tried to unite Cyprus to Greece in a failed coup. He sounded optimistic and told us about the continuing dialog between the respective presidents. The Turkish invasion was a bitter subject for my sister, Nouvart, ever since she and the boys (Ted being the oldest) had to evacuate their house because it was right on the border, and invaders were "at the doorstep." They were separated from her husband, Hercules, who was at his office in town. He was the minister of aviation, in the Cyprus government. The family was taken to a refugee camp in Dikkelia (a camp about ten miles beyond Larnaca, where the British maintained a military base) and for days they could not be reunited as a family. Because of these memories, she refused to go to the Turkish side, even after passage across the checkpoints was eased, and people could easily go back and forth.

While visiting with the Ambassador, I brought up another subject. Having come from Cyprus, and having my original passport still in my possession, what were the possibilities of reclaiming my citizenship? He assured me that there would be no problem at all in that regard. He then called an assistant to bring me the relevant application forms to fill and then assured me that it could be done within a year's time. He also assured me that not only I but my children could also become citizens! I came home thinking, "Well, maybe we can all retire there someday..." The papers remain on my desk partially filled out, however, waiting for my next move.

Looking back to the Panayiotides/Kassouni families' times together back in my adolescent years, one episode, among many, stands out and is worth telling. It happened when we were all gathered in their home, located at the corner of the Limassol and Nicosia roads, sometime in the mid-1940s. My sister, Agnes, Phoula's younger sister, Tilda, and I were playing in their back yard. We wandered outside the yard to the fields beyond. There was an old well there. It was not covered, and try as we did we could not see what was down below. Our curiosity drove us to come up with a bright idea. We gathered some newspapers, lighted them, and then threw them down the well to allow us see what was there. Very soon after, we got much more than we asked for. Debris that had collected in it caught fire! We almost panicked, thinking a big fire was soon to follow, but we still had enough sense to do something about it fast. We ran to the house, filled buckets with water, and poured the water into the well to snuff out the fire. We were successful, to our great relief! The interesting part about this episode is that we did all this without the rest of the family, who were inside the house, ever sensing something was wrong.

This trip was taken because I did not know if I would ever have the chance to travel east again. There was much nostalgia, included in why we went. These were heart-wrenching experiences for me, bringing back vivid memories of wonderful times spent together in Cyprus.

However, the sweet always accompanies the bitter, and it was no different on these trips. My nephews (four of them: Haig and his wife, Ann; Armen and his wife, Kim; Van and his wife Luba; Dicran, nicknamed "the Bee") and their families in Grand Rapids, Michigan, are amazing people of high motivation and accomplishment. Mingling our laughter with our tears, we celebrated Olivette's life, first with prayers and eulogies, and later with a beer or two.

The spring of 2016 was a happy one for my family in northern California, and a distinct joy for me as a father and grand-father. My pride and joy in seeing them blossom and bloom in personal, academic, and career-related changes are tempered only by my separation from them throughout the year. There is a deep-seated ache in my heart that is constant. It is a separation caused by my divorce, and I know in a way that it is God's judgment on me. Even though my children are very warm, accepting, and devoted to both Samira and me, the geographic separation forced on us by our continuing work and career in southern California, has maintained a chasm between us. Yes, we pass over that chasm from time to time in trips and visits up north, but those short visits, like the one last spring, cannot even begin to fill the void and sense of separation I feel constantly. In that regard I envy Addie, my former wife, who lives among the children, in Elk Grove, and has had the joys accompanying close family relations.

Having said that, I in no way feel alienated from my family in terms of love and emotional bonds. They are there for us all the time, and they do their best to keep our bonds strong and constant. Above it all, God's love continues to renew and bless us, and my ministry continues in the guidance and power of God's Spirit.

November 8, 2016, was a day when we shed tears of frustration and shock. Of course, we are referring to the election of Donald Trump to the presidency of our country. Samira and I were vacationing in Maui, Hawaii at the time. We stayed up very late the night before tracking the progress of the election results but went to bed before it was final, and hoping a miracle would have changed things overnight. To our, and many others', chagrin and deep dismay, the final word was out, that Donald Trump was elected. I include this matter in my memoirs because I believe that this was a watershed event that will change the direction and nature of our country for a long time, if not forever. A tectonic shift has occurred, which does not portend good for us all.

In that regard, I share with you what I read early that morning for my devotional. My New Testament (Eugene Peterson's version, the Message) fell open to the page where the ribbon had been placed long ago. My eyes were immediately drawn to 2 Timothy 3: paragraph 1, titled, "Difficult Times Ahead":

"Don't be naïve. There are difficult times ahead. As the end approaches, people are going to be self-absorbed, money hungry, self-promoting, stuck-up, profane, contemptuous of parents, crude, coarse, dog-eat-dog, unbending, slanderers…they'll make a show of religion…Stay clear of these people."

From what we have seen and heard about Mr. Trump, much of this description fits his way of doing things. Maybe so, and I hope, I am wrong in this regard. However, the opening sentence is right on: *"There are difficult times ahead."*

We have not yet recovered from our shock! Samira's comment was, "I want to sue Mr. Trump for spoiling our vacation!" As changes develop in how our government responds to the needs and challenges of our times, I pray we will react with positive and healthy responses. But what those will be remains to be seen.

And Beyond

Beyond this point, I am in God's hands. We have looked back over eighty-five years and traced God's guidance and direction, taking me from a tiny island to an arena of service literally including the whole world. It is my prayer that the influence I've had in the lives of people, near and far, will reflect the love of God as revealed in Christ, and that they carry on their mission in life for the good of all.

I'm not done yet! The years ahead, if God allows, will include more writing to share my views, convictions, observations, and theological reflections. Looking back, I am profoundly grateful for all who have touched my life and helped me to go a little further than I ever could on my own. God bless them all!

Celebrating the Kassouni Clan

A gathering of the Kassouni clan at my home, with my sister Nouvart Kassouni Djaferis *(front row, center)* and our cousin Aznive Meykhanejian, daughter of my mother's sister *(between Nouvart and me)*. Nouvart and Aznive are both now with the Lord. Orange, California, ca. 2005.

Celebrating Nouvart and Hercules' Djaferis' 50th Anniversary in the resort town of Agros. This is an historic photo as *(back row, left to right)* my brother Sarkis, Euclid Payayiotides-Dhjaferis, Hercules Panayiotides-Djaferis, and my sister Nouvart are all no longer with us. Sarkis' wife Olivette *(front row, first on left)* is also now gone. Also pictured *(back row)* are me and the Rev. Allan Viller; *(front row, remaining left to right)* Phoula Panayiotides Henry, Samira Kassouni, and Tilda Panayiotides Viller. This was the last time we were all together for a photo. Rodon Hotel, Cyprus, July 1999.

The three Kassounis together in 1999. Sorely missed was my sister Agnes.

The three Kassounis with Nouvart's husband Hercules.

In front of the school house in the village of Lefkara, Cyprus,
used to house our Academy when we had to evacuate Larnaca during World War II.

Visiting Friends and Family

Nancy McGinnis *(front)* with her cousins at the memorial celebration
of Olivette Kassouni, Greenville, Michigan, June 27, 2016.

With my four nephews (Sarkis and Olivette's sons) at the memorial celebration.
From left to right: Dicran, Van, Haig, me, and Armen.

At home with my good friend, Rev. John Markarian,
a renowned teacher-theologian-preacher-educator in the PC(USA).
He is only 99 in this photo! West Pittston, Pennsylvania, June 29, 2016.

1. Visiting the home of brother-in-law Richard and sister Agnes Scribner. *From right to left:* my nephew Ted Payayiotides- Djaferis (co-driver on the trip), Richard Scribner, his son Daniel Kassouni Scribner, his grandson Daniel Hunt Scribner, and me. Willow Street, Pennsylvania.
2. A rare opportunity for me to visit with my sister Agnes, living at the care facility in Willow Street, as she has been ailing for a number of years.
3. Ariadne Henry (Phoula's daughter), Ted, and me, on the steps of their home. Washington, DC, July 1, 2006.

Family Memories

1. Richard and Agnes Kassouni Scribner, ca. 1960s.
2. The three Kassounis in America: Sarkis, Agnes, and Vartkes, ca. 1957.
3. Agnes Kassouni Scribner, Olivette Kassouni, and Adrine Kassouni, ca. 1957.
4. Agnes and Richard with their first child, David, 1960.
5. Manuel and Martha Kassouni with grandsons David and Daniel Scribner, 1963.

And Beyond...

And now it's time
to say goodbye.

Acknowledgments

This book was written over the space of four years. It would not have been possible without the contribution of a number of people, named and unnamed. Their suggestions, encouragements, observations, and support. My deep gratitude goes to them all. My special thanks goes to **Loretta Herter,** who is herself a published author. She graciously agreed to be my editor and spent many hours reading and editing my manuscript. This she did over and over, correcting my script, suggesting changes and encouraging me on until its completion. She and her husband **Gerald** have been our friends for many years in our life together at Tustin Presbyterian Church. I am also indebted to **Patty Sanchez,** the receptionist at Tustin Presbyterian Church, for her ready support in matters of computer glitches, "lost" manuscripts, and retyping them as needed. A profound word of thanks goes to **Lori Schmalenberger**, who has provided invaluable service by taking charge of the photographs and organizing them into their final form for this book. Without her help I would not have been able to finalize this project. She and her husband, **Russell**, have also for many years been friends and colleagues in service at Tustin Presbyterian Church.

One other person who contributed much to the successful completion of this project was **Arthur Salibian, MD**. Along with reading the manuscript and making valuable suggestions, he is the artist who painted the front cover of this book as a most special favor to me.

Through it all, my constant companion and support has been **Samira,** my dear wife. Along with everything else, she put up with me when I closeted myself for long hours in my study and was oblivious to what was going on outside.

Thank you all!

Appendix 1

REFLECTIONS AND CONVICTIONS
(Developed in eighty years of life and ministry)

On the occasion of my eightieth birthday I have jotted down some thoughts. I pass them on hoping they will be of some service to my readers in their own life and faith journey.

On Birth:

They tell me I was born eighty years ago on January 18. I take their word for it because I don't remember the event. However, accompanying and subsequent events have confirmed that to be true. Thank you, Manuel and Martha. People tell me you did a "good job." Birth is totally a gift, generated by parents, and in the case of spiritual birth, a gift from God. Whether one is "alive" spiritually or not does not depend on whether one remembers dates but on whether one demonstrates the existence of life generated by the Spirit of God. Thank you God!

On Faith:

As the years have passed, I have moved from a position of claiming to be a "true believer" based on "orthodox" doctrinal assertions concerning God, Jesus Christ, and the Bible. Instead, I have grown in understanding and experience that faith is essentially trust. To illustrate this truth,

I have often talked of walking in the dark unlighted streets of my home town at night when as a boy in Larnaca, Cyprus. Faith as trust meant walking next to my dad who led the way and knew where we were going, with my hand in his great coat pocket lined with velvet! I felt secure not because I knew but because I trusted. So it is with Christian faith. Led by the Good Shepherd, we accept life in faith and walk trusting him who said, "I am the Way, the Truth, the Life."

On the Bible:

Over the years, I have watched in amazement and listened with un-belief, as Christians have turned against each other claiming to have a superior view of the Bible. The Book has replaced the Person, and fights have replaced fellowship in Christ. How tragic!

The Bible is a compilation of books stretched over centuries in their origin, which contain for the reader acts and events initiated, led, and inspired by God, with commentary following. It begins with Creation, and ends with the Revelation of God in the person of Jesus Christ. The Word written (the Bible) is the witness to the Word living (Jesus Christ). The Book is not inerrant in any and all subject matters it contains. Its inerrancy is found in not only the leading of the readers, by the Holy Spirit, to consider and receive the gift of Life, revealed in many events recorded therein, but ultimately in the person and teach-ings of Jesus Christ. To use the Bible in any other fashion is to misuse it. I have observed over the years that misuse of Scripture leads to abuse of people. Hence we have among us the accusations, the fights, the separations within the Body of Christ, the Church.

On Identity:

Who am I? By ethnic identity, I am Armenian. By national identity, I am American. By spiritual identity, I am Christian. Within the triangle formed by these three key points of identity, my life has experienced meaning, guidance, and vocation. Central to it all has been Love: of parents and siblings; of teachers and pastors; of family and friends; of colleagues in ministry. I have been and continue to be proud of them all, and I thank them for being there for me, and for shaping who I am with such clarity and purpose. Love, support, and joys have flown my way from my family in particular for all these many years. My four children and their mother have been special indeed. Eight precious grandchildren continue to add great dimensions of pride and joy in my life. My wife, Samira, is "something else." This celebration of my birthday which she has planned and accomplished is an example of how she brings joy into my life daily. My only regret is that I have at times failed to return the love of all these dear people and have been ungrateful and selfish. I ask their forgiveness.

Within the framework of these realities, I have lived in wonder and awe, moving from country to country, from city to city, from people to people, from church to church. Everywhere I've gone I have been surprised by God's loving hand, bringing to me people of many nationalities, ethnic origins, national aspirations, and spiritual insight. I have looked to them all as messengers of God to help me move one more step forward, to live one day longer, to enlarge my borders one more mile. Along the way, I have grown not only in understanding my own identity but the identity of God as well.

On God:

God remains to be, for me, a reality beyond my ability to define or comprehend but to accept and worship in awe. Awe leaves us speechless, and that is how authentic worship happens—in silence! The prophet says, "Be still and know that I am God." God has grasped me and continues to do so, but I can never grasp God, or hold God within the limits of my mind, my traditions, my belief system, or my identity. Those (people and religions) who claim they do so, actually do nothing more than attempt to shape God in their own image, and then they often use their "God" to oppress others who do not accept their beliefs. A favorite verse of mine says, "God was in Christ reconciling the world unto himself." God seeks reconciliation and peace. Instead of peace, abusers of the term "God" use it for separation and war!

I have no problem, as a believer, in accepting science and affirming my faith as well. In my own rather simple way (hopefully not simplistic), I define God in terms Jesus used, "God is Spirit." Then, I listen to science that defines "energy" as the essence of life. Faith, then defines energy as Spirit, and the difference is personality. Energy is Power, and Spirit is energy that relates power to person. So God is not just "Force" (with my apologies to Star Wars) but my Heavenly Father. We do not say, "May the Force be with you" but "May God be with you." Thus, faith makes the difference.

On the Future:

The Psalmist says that "seventy years is all that we have—eighty years, if we are strong." Well, having reached eighty makes me wonder: How long will my strength last? Again, I confess I am in God's hands, and I take life as a gift, from day to day. From my house we can view only sunrises and not sunsets. That for me is symbolic of life. View the sunrises and be thankful that you can! Yesterday, the sunrise was glorious. I grabbed my camera and photographed it. I certainly hope to see many more sunrises, each promising for me another day filled with surprises of joy and of sorrow, of laughter and of tears. So be it.

The Psalmist also says, "Teach us how short life is, so that we may become wise." How many more years left for me? I don't know, but I pray they may be years spent in loving relationship with you and all others around me in the love and grace of our Lord Jesus Christ.

–Vartkes "Kass" Kassouni, January 18, 2011, revised February 8, 2017

Appendix 2

TEXT OF A LETTER OF COMMENDATION FROM
DR. BOB JONES JR.

BOB JONES University
Greenville • South Carolina
December 15, 1953

Mr. Vartkes Kassouni
Biblical Seminary in New York
235 West 49th Street
New York 17, New York

Dear Vartkes:

I just returned to the campus from Oskaloosa, Iowa, where I was
for an evangelistic campaign. We had a good time out there and
are thankful for the Lord's blessings.

While I was away, Dr. D.A. Berberian of Loudonville, New York,
wrote and mentioned what a blessing you and some of the other
boys had been to the young people in Lebanon and Syria. (He
was there this past summer on his way to Turkey for a medical

meeting.) He said that you, Al Finley, Dick Knox, and Morris Hanna were mentioned by so many boys and girls, many of whom were led to the Lord through the ministry of you boys, and that these young people are now actively at work in their respective churches and Christian Endeavor organizations. Of course, we are pleased to have this good word about the work you did there, and I thought it would be an encouragement to you to know that your ministry is still bearing fruit.

We are having a wonderful year and the Lord is blessing abundantly. Be assure of our prayers for you. Kind regards.

Your friend,
Bob Jones Jr.
President

Appendix 3

A HYMN BY DR. DAVID GAMBRELL.
Reprinted by permission.

Lord, to You Our People Cry

a hymn in solemn commemoration of the 100th anniversary of the Armenian Genocide

Lord, to you our people cry; heavy hearts and
Ev - en now, a - cross the years, we re - call those
Lord, re - store us; make us new. Give us life and

spir - its sigh. See what e - vil we have known,
days with tears. Ev - en now, with grief, we see
hope in you. Let the ways of vio - lence cease;

forced up - on our flesh and bone: driv - en from our
pres - ent pain and cru - el - ty. Make us bold to
bless the ones who seek your peace. Shine with love in

na - tive land, swept a - way, like des - ert sand.
act and speak when the strong op - press the weak.
ev - ery place, Sun of jus - tice, Light of grace.

Text: David Gambrell, 2015; inspired by Gregory of Narek (951–1003)
Tune: ARFON 7.7.7.7.7.7; French and Welsh melody; arr. Hugh Davies, 1906
The first and last phrases of this text are inspired by the opening and closing prayers of the Book of
Lamentations by Gregory of Narek (Grigor Narekatsi), a tenth-century Armenian monk and poet.

Author Biography

Vartkes M. Kassouni was born the youngest of four children on the island of Cyprus, where his Armenian parents immigrated in 1921. His education began at a missionary school. After coming to America in 1949, he attended Bob Jones University. He also holds a master of divinity degree from New York Theological Seminary and a doctor of ministry degree from McCormick Theological Seminary.

He has spent his career with the Presbyterian Church. Though his ministry has taken place in central and southern California, as a church developer, Kassouni was the initiating pastor of new churches in Laguna Niguel, Rancho Santa Margarita, Yorba Linda, and North Huntington Beach. In these ministries, his biggest feats have been to reach past ethnocentric community walls and to embrace a more inclusive theology.

Kassouni has four children and eight grandchildren. He has lived with his wife, Samira, in Orange, California, since their marriage in 1987.

Made in the USA
Lexington, KY
11 September 2017